Seeking
the Face
of God

Seeking
the Face
of God

William H. Shannon

CROSSROAD · NEW YORK

1988

The Crossroad Publishing Company
370 Lexington Avenue, New York, N.Y. 10017

Copyright © 1988 by William H. Shannon

Printed in the United States of America

Library of Congress Cataloging-in-Publication Data

Shannon, William Henry, 1917–
    Seeking the face of God : an approach to Christian prayer and
spirituality / William H. Shannon.
    p.   cm.
    Bibliography: p.
    ISBN 0-8245-0883-1
    1. Prayer.   2. Spiritual life—Catholic authors.   I. Title.
BV210.2.S477 1988   87-32942
248.3—dc 19   CIP

To my students —
the alumnae and alumni
of Nazareth College of Rochester.

During my tenure of almost forty years
they taught me more than I know.

Contents

Preface

At one point in the writing of this book I had thought I might call it *Thomas Merton's Tiger Lilies*. Though I eventually rejected this title, the experience that suggested it may be of interest. Several years ago I had the rare privilege of making a retreat at the little cinder-block cottage, in the woods near the Abbey of Gethsemani, that once served as Thomas Merton's hermitage. I arrived on a beautiful Kentucky blue-sky afternoon and, to my delight, found that I was welcomed not only by my good friend Brother Patrick Hart, but also by a bed of sturdy tiger lilies in full bloom next to the tiny chapel that is attached to the hermitage.

I settled down in the hermitage looking forward to a week of quiet and reflection. Evening and morning came the first day and I found myself fascinated by the evening and morning ritual of the tiger lilies. Each evening, as the sun settled behind the woods and dusk covered the valley, they slowly closed their petals, turning in on themselves for the time of night's darkness. Then in the morning, as the sun sparkled the dew-filled valley, they gently opened their petals to the outside world and resumed their appointed task of adorning God's creation with their own touch of beauty.

The lesson of that daily ritual was not a difficult one to learn. The rhythm of going within oneself alternating with a turning out to the world is the rhythm of any true spirituality. We need to turn within to find God and our own true selves and the great wide world finding its roots in Him; and we need also to turn outward to carry out our appointed task in an often broken world: the task of healing, reconciling, making whole, bringing the Gospel of justice and love and peace to those who long for compassion and freedom.

The present work is about that "going in" and "coming out" that any commitment to prayer and spirituality demands. All I really want to say is what the tiger lilies say, though my many words will never match the eloquence of their silent rhythm. The words will tell how one person discovered the Christian tradition in his own experience. I want to say from the start, therefore, that this book will be mildly, though I hope fairly unobtrusively, autobiographical. I choose to write this way not because I think that my story is particularly *unique* (though I suppose that every story is in some sense unique), but because I think it is *typical*. If this is so, then perhaps others may find that somehow it articulates, or helps them to articulate, their own story. The stories divine grace writes in different lives are perhaps much more alike than we have realized. This may dawn on those who have the courage to make their way through the rest of this book.

1

Seeking the Face of God

For the last dozen years or so I have devoted much of my time and energies to studying and writing about Thomas Merton. I want to say at the outset that this book is not about Thomas Merton. It is a book about prayer and more specifically about contemplation. It would of course be silly for a person who had spent a dozen years studying Merton to write a book about contemplation and say that Merton had nothing to do with it. Obviously much of what I will say will be colored, consciously or not, by what I have read about contemplation in the works of Thomas Merton. On occasion I shall quote from Merton and will try honestly to acknowledge his influence whenever I feel that it is his thought that I am presenting. Yet I want to take personal responsibility for this book. I want it to be, as far as possible, what I have to say about prayer. Whether what I have to say about prayer is important to or helpful for anyone but myself is, of course, for the readers to judge. All I can say in justification for writing it is that doing a book on prayer at this present time represents a need in me. I feel like Master Eckhart (and I think I'm remembering this from Merton—here I go already!) who once said that if he had prepared a sermon and went into a church and found it empty, he would nonetheless go ahead and deliver the sermon. No publisher is going to want me to say this, but I experience something like a call to write a book on prayer, even if nobody ever reads it.

One simple way to write a book on prayer would be to produce a book with a title page that would be followed by a hundred or more blank pages, with just the invitation at the beginning: "Go through these pages slowly and silently." Such a book would be an invitation to revel in silence, to open oneself up to the creativity of silence. If a person were to take this invitation seriously, it might open him or her to the experience of how "productive" silence can be.

Silence: A Hidden Hunger

Many people would probably find it difficult to read such a book. Our lives are so cluttered with words that we don't know how to handle silence well. So how could we possibly deal with a book that has no text? How could we ever make sense out of reading a book with no words? We have long since accepted as a fact that it is not by bread alone that people live, but by words. In our society, at least for many people in it, silence is not seen as a value, but simply as the fruitless and sometimes uncomfortable pause between words. We are a society of men and women sated with words and starved for silence. But we do not realize that silence is what we need, and so the little silence we have we fill with the noise of our stereos and our televisions. The picture of a young man or woman walking down the street with earplugs reaching from their pocket stereos into their ears and shutting out not so much the common noise that is outside but the fruitful possibility of silence that could be inside may serve as a mirror of our age. It is an age wherein words and noises conspire to block silence out of our lives, and all too often we ourselves are parties to the conspiracy.

During World War II, when our cities were blacked out at night, it was thought advisable to move some of the children of New York City to the relative safety of the Catskill Mountains. When they first arrived in the quiet stillness of the country, they were unable to sleep—because it was too quiet. So accustomed had they become to the noises of the city that the silence of the open country kept them awake. They could not relax with silence. This might be read as a parable of today's society: It images our uncomfortableness with silence. We cannot relax with it either. When we are at a party and there is a lull in the conversation, we reach desperately for more words to fill in the gap between words. Because we have not learned to live with silence, we resort to almost any device to avoid it.

Our age — the age of widespread and relentless media communication — needs, perhaps more than any earlier generation, to learn the meaning of silence and its place in our lives. Silence is the necessary ground for words that have something to say. Authentic silence is pregnant with words that will be born at the right time. But unless our words are born out of a reflective silence, they are apt to be curtains that cover reality rather than windows that reveal it. For silence can give us access to a dimension of reality that is too deep for words. That is why when we speak out of the experience of silence, there is always more experience left over. For you cannot say all that silence reveals to you. Words cannot hold the totality of your silence.

Silence is especially important if I want to learn to pray. For prayer at least at its deepest level is not so much conversation with God, but my silence communing with the silence of God. In this silent encounter I experience that God is ALL and that apart from God I am nothing. Hence I do not want to discard lightly the notion of a book about contemplation that would be a "book of no words." Reading through "not-reading" may well be the best way to come to understand what contemplation is.

But before one can read the "book of no words," it is probably necessary (or at least we would tend to think it is) to read the book of words. The first word I should like to say about contemplation is that it is, or can be, an experience for all of us. It is not an elitist enterprise. For Christians it is the normal flowering of our baptismal call to union with God. More and more people are beginning to realize this. Yet it remains true that for many Christians contemplation still has to be rescued from the marginal place it occupies in their lives and priorities. There are many who still believe that the closest they can come to contemplation is "saying their prayers" or "attending religious services." These people believe in God and are intent on doing His will; yet God remains for them a remote being whose presence must be mediated for them. Thus they believe that God's existence can be proved, that He governs the universe and saves us by His grace. But they are more comfortable experiencing His action in their lives through the medium of the Church: her preaching and her sacraments.

A "Mediated" Experience of God — Is It Enough?

What this means is that for many Christians the Church and its activities appear to be more important to them than God. Or, to put it another way, they prefer to be in touch with God through a "third party." They are like the people of Israel, standing at the foot of Mt. Sinai and almost literally scared to death about approaching God and His Holy Mountain. That is why, as we are told in the Book of Exodus, they took a position far away from the Mountain and said to Moses: "You speak to us and we will listen; but let not God speak to us, or we shall die" (Exod. 20:18–19). They want no direct contact with God. Let Moses be the intermediary. In similar fashion, many Christians prefer the mediation of the Church to any kind of direct experience of God. Such direct experience will have to wait for the life to come. It is an eschatological reality. "To see God" is to be in heaven; being *here* means not "seeing" God, not experiencing Him. "Saying our prayers," participating in the sacraments, trying to live lives of virtue — these are the faith realities of this life. To experience God is for later, not for now.

Or if it is for now, it is for an elitist group. For a long time that elitist group was considered to be monks, priests, and religious. Most people could not have an experience of God this side of the eschatological divide, but maybe these "special people" could.

A Personal Confession

The difficulty has been that these "special people" — many of them at least — did not think of themselves as any more capable of experiencing God than any of the "nonspecial" people. If I may take myself as an example, I spent a good deal of my life worrying about the fact that I didn't know how to pray very well. In fact, I considered myself a downright failure at prayer. It wasn't that I didn't try. I did. In fact (as I came to learn later), that was the problem: I tried too hard. And if you try too hard to pray, you will almost certainly end up thinking that you are rather poor at prayer.

I spent six years in a Roman Catholic major seminary. These were the years when I expected I would learn to pray. After all, the seminary was supposed to be training me to be a priest. One of the things a priest was expected to do was to teach people how to pray.

I didn't learn to pray the first year I was there. So I supposed it would happen in the second or third year. But it didn't. Not in the fourth or fifth either. At the end of the sixth year, I was ready for ordination and it still hadn't happened. I was going to be ordained a priest and I didn't know how to pray. I was ordained and assigned to a parish, and I thought to myself: "People will expect me to teach them how to pray. What am I going to do? I cannot teach them to do what I can't do myself."

As far as contemplation was concerned, that was something completely out of the question. I knew that I was no John of the Cross: I certainly wasn't ready to ascend Mt. Carmel. I didn't even know where it was. True, I had taken a course in mystical theology in seminary. It was one hour per week for one year (whereas classes in dogmatic theology and moral theology were five times a week for four years — which was some gauge of the relative importance attached to mystical theology). Actually, in terms of time commitment, mystical theology was on a par with the seminary course we took on keeping parish books (a course we dubbed "sacred arithmetic"). It too was one hour per week for one year. One of the things it taught us was how to balance a bank book. I never had a bank book till after I was ordained, and fortunately my assignments were such that I never had to handle any parish books. I say "fortunately" because I have never been able to balance my personal check book.

This meant that two of the things I was supposed to know how to do after I left the seminary I actually wasn't able to do: I wasn't able to balance a check book and I wasn't able to pray.

I will say that I tried harder in the mystical theology course than I did in "sacred arithmetic." I read such people as Garrigou-Lagrange who wrote about natural contemplation and supernatural or infused contemplation. You would have thought I would have made out all right at least with *natural* contemplation, but actually I didn't. There were a lot of things that came to me quite naturally (like smoking cigars and drinking martinis) but — sad to say — contemplation didn't seem to be one of them. And as for *infused* contemplation, I was quite sure that when I tried to pray, nothing at all was being "infused" into me, certainly not contemplation.

I remember how as a young priest I used to go to a Jesuit retreat house for an annual retreat. The retreat-master gave four conferences each day, each of them lasting for about twenty-five minutes. Then the idea was to spend the remaining thirty-five minutes of each hour's prayer-time in personal mediation on what had been said in the conference. I tried. After about ten minutes, I had used up all that he had said and still had a good twenty-five minutes to go. So I gritted my teeth and stayed there for the rest of the hour, sneaking a somewhat guilty look at my watch every few minutes with the hope — I wouldn't always admit it to myself — that the hour would soon be over.

All the while I was quite sure of one thing: that I really wasn't praying; or, at the very least, that I wasn't praying very well.

I don't know whether this sort of thing was something that was happening to others. I never dared to talk with anyone about it (because I couldn't bear to admit to anyone that I didn't know how to pray). One thing I do know: I have on occasion known people who boasted, one way or another, about their talents. But I have never heard anyone boast about his or her prayer. I have never heard anyone say: "Oh, yes, I pray very well." I have a strong suspicion that the vast majority of people, if you were to ask them to evaluate their prayer-life, would say: "I don't really pray very well." And they would really mean it. It would not be like other situations that might come up in which people might think it proper to make a self-derogatory statement. For instance, you might say to someone: "You certainly play the piano well" or "Your art work is sensational." And they might reply: "That's kind of you. But I'm not really that good at it." They would say something like that because they figured that modesty required that they say it. But what they are really saying inside is: "You better believe it. I really do play well." Or "I really am a fine artist." But—at least I believe this—when people say: "I don't pray well," you know they really mean it. It is not a false modesty. It's just what they think is true. They really do not believe that they pray well.

I think anyway that this would be true about most people—this feeling of inadequacy in prayer. I certainly know it was true about me. And it was most frustrating: something like being a French teacher and not knowing any French or being a math teacher and not knowing how to add or subtract. It made you feel like a phony. You were made a priest, in part at least, to teach people how to pray. And you couldn't pray (so you thought) if your life depended on it.

Eventually a couple of things happened to me that transformed my understanding of prayer, and especially of contemplation; they helped to clear up some of the confusion I had not been able to deal with and to recover from the frustrations about prayer I had been laboring under.

Paul's Epistle to the Romans and Prayer

One of the things that happened to me is that at a certain time in my life I was suddenly hit over the head — or in the head or, maybe better, in the heart, which alone really understands the things of God — by something that St. Paul said in his Epistle to the Romans. Romans seems to be a book that has bowled over quite a number of people at various times. In the fifth century Augustine went to it and found there his doctrine of original sin. In the sixteenth century Martin Luther learned from Romans his teaching about salvation through faith alone. And in the twentieth century it was Karl Barth's giant commentary on Romans that changed the direction of theological thought. With absolutely no modesty at all, I add myself to these giants (with whom obviously I do not belong) and say that it was in the second half of the twentieth century that I found a text in Romans that was vital to my understanding of myself, my prayer, my approach to contemplation.

The statement of St. Paul that exercised such a transforming effect on me can be found in verses 26 and 27 of chapter 8:

> [T]he Spirit too comes to the aid of our weakness; for we do not know how to pray as we ought, but the Spirit itself intercedes with inexpressible groanings. And the one who searches hearts knows what is the intention of the Spirit, because it intercedes for the holy ones according to God's will. (New American Bible, rev. ed.)

If that bit about the Spirit interceding for us with a lot of "groaning" gets to you, you might find yourself more comfortable (as I did) with the translation in the New English Bible, in which the "groanings" are attributed, more fittingly so it seems, to us (and this is a legitimate way of reading the Greek text). The NEB translation has it this way:

> The Spirit comes to the aid of our weakness. We do not even know how we ought to pray, but through our inarticulate groans the Spirit Himself is pleading for us, and God who searches our inmost being knows what the Spirit means, because He pleads for God's own people in God's own way.

But whichever translation you use, the point is very clear when all of a sudden you finally get it. And it took me a long time "to get it." I suppose I must have read that text many times. Then one day, all at once, the words leaped out from the page. I heard Paul saying (and it's there in both translations): "we don't know how we ought to pray."

It was as if I had suddenly, unaccountably, met St. Paul and blurted out to him: "Paul, my good friend, I have been working at it all my life and I don't know how to pray." And in my "vision" I saw him smile and heard him say: "Yes, of course. That's true, isn't it? You don't know how to pray. Well, join the crowd. We all have the same problem, don't we? But the answer is not to try to find somebody who will teach you how to pray. The answer to your problem is to let go your desire to pray and let God pray in you. Just be attentive to and aware of God's Presence. The Spirit who is in you will do the praying. That is what matters. Stop trying to do a lot of things that will make you think that you are praying. Because if you think you have to do a lot of things in prayer, that will make it difficult for God to do things in you in prayer. Be quiet and silent. Let 'prayer' pray in you."

This was the Pauline thunderbolt that hit me. Paul was telling me that I didn't have to be concerned about this problem that had been vexing me for so long a time. I had been saying all along that *I could not pray* and all along *prayer was happening in me.* What I needed most was to be silent and truly aware of what was going on in me.

This was a great insight and I can't say how much peace it brought. I suspect, however, that such an insight might not have come to me if I had not, at the same time, been deeply into what Thomas Merton had to say about prayer. (And here I want obviously to acknowledge my debt to him.) It is very congenial to Merton's thought on prayer to state that there is a sense in which it is very true to say that we don't pray, but rather we let prayer happen in us. The best we can do is to prepare and dispose ourselves to let it happen.

Thomas Merton and His Personal Prayer

Though Merton has a great deal to say about prayer in his various books and essays (indeed, toward the end of his life he said he wished he hadn't written so much on prayer), he tends to be quite reticent about his personal prayer. There is one remarkable exception. In a letter to his Sufi friend in Pakistan, Abdul Aziz, Merton—in response to Abdul Aziz's persistent questioning—does speak of his own way of prayer. He writes:

> Strictly speaking I have a very simple way of prayer. It is centered entirely on attention to the presence of God and to His will and His love.

This, he makes clear, is a matter of *faith*, by which alone we can know the presence of God. In clarifying what he means by "attention to the presence of God," he uses the words of the Prophet Muhammad and says with him that it is like "being before God as if you saw Him." Merton hastens to make clear that he does not mean having "a precise image of God" that you can imagine. This, he says, would be idolatry. Hence prayer is "a matter of adoring Him as invisible and infinitely beyond our comprehension."

Merton goes on to link his prayer with a fundamental notion

that belongs to Sufi prayer: "My prayer tends very much toward what you call *fana*." *Fana*, I might say, is a difficult term to understand. Literally, it means to be absorbed in God. It means to lose oneself in God. Of course another way to saying the same thing is "to find oneself in God." What do we find when we find ourselves in God? We really find God. But I go on with Merton's words, in which he explains what *fana* means to him:

> There is in my heart this great thirst to recognize totally the nothingness of all that is not God. My prayer is then a kind of praise rising up out of the center of Nothing and Silence.

Notice that the prayer arises from what he calls the center of Nothing and Silence. It does not arise from the ego-self. Merton makes this very explicit:

> If I am still present "myself," this I recognize as an obstacle about which I can do nothing unless He Himself removes the obstacle.

He makes two further statements: one that expresses the joy of prayer, the other its frustration:

> If He wills He can make the Nothingness into a total clarity. If He does not will, then the Nothingness seems to itself to be an *object* and remains an obstacle. Such is my ordinary prayer.

Finally, he points out that his prayer involves not a use of imagination and reason, but a quieting of them. "It is not," he says, "thinking about *anything*, but a direct seeking of the Face of the Invisible, which cannot be found unless we become lost in Him who is Invisible" (*The Hidden Ground of Love*, pp. 63–64).

I think Merton is telling us that prayer does not mean trying to find God, much less trying to find ourselves. Rather it is "getting lost" in God. And isn't this another way of saying what that passage from Romans 8 said: We don't know how to pray, but we don't have to; for it is God, God's Spirit, who prays in us. Prayer happens when we allow ourselves (or at least dispose ourselves) to be aware of the presence of God or—the same thing—to get lost in Him/Her. Sometimes, when we want to dismiss someone, we may use the expression "Get lost." When we say "get lost" to our ego-self, we realize that we are in God. We become aware of God's presence.

To become aware of God's presence is to become aware of what is always there. We are always in God. We are not always aware that we are in God. The intent of this book is to show that the chief purpose of prayer is to achieve and to deepen that awareness. One of the theses of this book, therefore, will be that we do not have to get anywhere in prayer. We do not have to get anywhere because we are already there. We do have to be aware that we are there.

The "Face" of God

I want to pick up briefly on Merton's rather curious statement that his prayer is "not thinking about anything, but a *direct seeking of the Face of the Invisible.*" At first reading these words appear paradoxical, if not downright contradictory. He is talking about prayer that eschews thinking and imagining, yet he ends up describing it in terms that suggest thinking and imagining: "a direct seeking of the Face of the Invisible." In understanding these words, it is important to remember that all language we use about God is symbolic and metaphorical. We can describe how we experience God only in words that describe our experience of what belongs to the created order. We have no "God-language," only human language that is always inadequate to describe the divine reality.

There are, however, certain symbols that recur again and again in religious language. One such symbol is that of the "Face" as symbolizing God's Being, existence, presence. It is an appropriate symbol: for when we meet someone it is the person's face that makes him or her most immediately present to us. The face is the most expressive part of our physical being, registering and revealing our thoughts and emotions. It is something seen that tells us about what is unseen, something visible that points to that which is invisible.

If I may invite you to think the absurd for a moment, imagine what it would be like for a teacher to enter a classroom and see before him/her twenty people—but each without a face. The experience, to put it mildly, would be eerie and disorienting. Lecturing in such a situation would mean, in effect, an attempt to speak to a group of "nobodies." To imagine a person without a face is to think of someone without an identity. For the face is the outward expression of who we are. It is what makes me most vividly present to others.

Seeing the "Face" of God as a synonym for experiencing God's presence is a consistent theme in the Psalms. Indeed, in the Old Testament seeing the "Face" of God is described as an experience that is at once fascinating and terrifying. It fascinates: people yearn to see the "Face" of God; yet at the same time it terrifies: there is the deep intuition that to see the "Face" of God means to die. This fascination for the "Face" of God is also true of Islam. God's "Face" is spoken of in the Koran in a number of places. Thus in Sura 28 we read: "Everything perishes but His Face." Al-Ghazali, a noted Muslim mystic of the eleventh century, commenting on this verse from the Koran, writes:

Everything hath two faces, a face of its own, and a face of its Lord; in respect of its own face it is nothingness, and in respect of the Face of God it is Being.

This quotation (taken from Martin Ling's book *A Sufi Saint of the Twentieth Century*, which he was reading in 1967) Merton connects, in one of his reading notebooks, with an unidentified Muslim hadith that says:

> God hides himself behind seventy-thousand veils of light and darkness. If he took away the veils, the penetrating light of his Face would at once destroy the sight of any creature who dares to look at it.

Merton comments, with some enthusiasm, on this hadith:

> And of course, if He took away the veils, there would be no choice but to "look at" His Face, for one would see it unveiled in oneself. One would no longer "be" a veil but "be" the Face. Total disappearance of the non-face. Would this be so "terrible"? Let it come!

The underlying theme of this book — that we are in God and that the goal of prayer is to become aware of this fact — can be aptly expressed through the symbol of the "Face." To experience the "Face" of God is to experience His "presence." Before we can experience the "Face" (the presence), however, we have to remove the veils that come between us and the "Face." If the goal of prayer, then, is to see the "Face" of God, the task of prayer is to remove the veils that prevent us from seeing. The God of the "Face," therefore, is the God who reveals Himself/Herself to us, that is to say, God removes the veils (this is the literal meaning of *revelare*) that prevent us from experiencing the Holy Presence. But if we are to meet the God of the "Face," we need to be clear where these veils are located and what they are. The veils are not in God, but in us. The Divine Being is translucent. It is our being that is veiled, that is beclouded by illusions that hide reality: not only God's reality, but our own and that of the world. Veiled in illusions, we cannot see what is actually present to us. Hence it is only when we have been "revealed," that is, stripped of the veils of our illusions so that we stand in utter poverty (which means total awareness) before the Invisible One, that the living God can "reveal" the fullness of His/ Her presence to us.

I have said that this is a book about prayer, which is to say that it is about awareness of God's presence and our need to be open to the experience of that awareness. It is, therefore, about the *task* of prayer: the steps we must take to remove the veils that shroud our vision. But especially it is about what is the *great adventure* of prayer: *seeking the Face of God*.

2

The Prayer of the Desert and the Prayer of the Choir

One deep realization that emerges from reading the Bible is the importance of prayer in the relationship between human persons and their Creator. In the Old Testament, not only is there an entire book made up exclusively of prayers (the Psalter), but in many ways much of the Old Testament may be seen as books of praise, repentance, and joy in the Lord that expressed the prayer-life of the people of Israel. Thus, for instance, what Scripture scholars call the Deuteronomic history (the books from Joshua through to the second book of Kings) — which tell the story of Israel from the entrance into the Promised Land to the loss of that land — may be seen as one long confession of sins laid at the feet of Israel's God and asking forgiveness and reconciliation. The fervor of prayer runs high in the Hebrew Scriptures.

The Prayer of Jesus
Prayer is also a central reality of the human encounter with God in the New Testament. Paul's Epistles frequently flow into prayer. One of the moving features of the Gospels is the frequency of references to the prayer of Jesus. Nowhere is this truer than in the Gospel of Luke, which has been rightly called "the Gospel of prayer." There can be no doubt that Jesus' unique

communing with his Father fascinated the Lukan author. The oneness of Jesus with the Father that is so clear in John's Gospel is surely implicit in Luke's; and it is a oneness that involves a special tenderness and a profound and unfathomable love. This, surely, is the reason why it is only from Luke that we receive the precious gift of that most exquisite of all parables — the prodigal son — which of course is really a parable about the loving Father, the Father of our Lord Jesus Christ and the Father of us all. We may ask too: does this fascination Luke has about Jesus' special relationship with his Father account for the fact that only he tells us that Jesus' last thoughts on the cross were about his Father? The other Gospel writers are content to say that at the end Jesus cried out with a loud voice. Only Luke tells us *what* he cried out before he breathed his last: "Father, into your hands I commend my spirit." For Luke Jesus' last act is prayer: that special communing with God that seemed to have gripped so strongly the attention of the author of our third Gospel.

It is not surprising, then, that for Luke important events in Jesus' life take place at times of prayer or are accompanied by prayer. The two key events in which his identity comes to be revealed — the baptism and the transfiguration — both highlight the prayer-context in which these events took place. At the baptism, it is while Jesus is *at prayer, after he had been baptized*, that "the Holy Spirit descends on him in visible form like a dove" and the voice from heaven is heard proclaiming him "beloved Son" (3:21). Again, at the transfiguration, it is *while he was praying* that his face changes in appearance and his clothes become dazzlingly white, as once again a voice from heaven gives testimony that he is indeed "Son" and "Chosen One" (9:35).

Momentous decisions in Jesus' ministry are also presented by Luke in the context of prayer. In chapter 6 we read that, before he chose the Twelve, "he went out to the mountain to pray, spending the night in communion with God" (v. 12). And when he puts to the disciples the question that will lead to

Peter's profession of faith in his messiahship, it is at a time when he is praying (Luke seems almost to suggest that the questioning was a part of the prayer): "One day when Jesus was praying in seclusion, and his disciples were with him, he put the question to them: "Who do the crowds say that I am?" (9:18). After they have offered various answers, Jesus goes on to ask them who they say that he is, and Peter confesses: "You are the Messiah of God."

The prayer of Jesus—one cannot help but wonder what it was like. While the Gospels speak of his prayer, they are generally quite reticent about its content. For the most part they draw a discreet curtain over Jesus' relation with his Father: what that relationship was and what it meant to Jesus no human words could ever convey. Better not to try. There are, however, a few instances, precious surely for the Christian community, wherein we are told things that he said in prayer; they seem to be confined mostly to the passion narratives (one of these I have already mentioned) and for the most part they are, significantly, prayers of intercession. The most moving perhaps (moving because we can easily see ourselves imaged in it) is the prayer in the Garden of Gethsemane: a prayer in which Jesus pleads with his· Father that the future may be different from what it appears it is going to be; at the same time it is a prayer of absolute resignation to the Father's will: "Father, if it is your will, take this chalice from me; yet not my will but yours be done." The Epistle to the Hebrews speaks in poignant terms of Jesus' intercessions with his Father.

> In the days when he was in the flesh, he offered prayers and supplications with loud cries and tears to God who was able to save him from death, and he was heard because of his reverence. (5:7)

That Jesus' prayer was distraught and agonizing at certain times, notably at the time of the passion, surely endears him to suffering humanity. Yet it would falsify the fundamental thrust of the Gospels to imply that this was the principal substance of his prayer. The tranquil serenity of Jesus that so clearly emerges from the pages of the Gospels would surely suggest that his prayer must have been, quite generally, a joyful communing in peace and love with the God whom he dared to call "Abba." Gilbert Keith Chesterton remarks somewhere that the Gospels never tell us that Jesus laughed. Chesterton suggests that the answer to this problem (if it is a problem) may be that Jesus saved his laughter for those glorious moments when he was alone with his Father, lost in prayer. This picture of Jesus roaring with laughter as he recounts the most recent antics of his disciples, while possibly appealing to some temperaments, seems overcolloquial (to say the least!), though perhaps it could represent a clumsy attempt to capture something of the spontaneity and intimacy of those timeless moments Jesus spent in communing with his Father.

Jesus' Oneness with the Father

One of the dangers in Chesterton's whimsical musing about Jesus "having a good laugh" with his Father is that it tends to distort the true meaning of that communing with God which is the deepest meaning of prayer. For it suggests a separateness of Jesus from the Father, as if Jesus were "here" and the Father "there," as if Jesus went into the desert to meet his Father at a specified place — somewhat as if I might arrange to meet my friend at the corner pub. Jesus met the Father within, in the depths of his own being. He was always present to the Father. His moments of prayer were special experiences of awareness of the ongoing reality that he was in the Father and the Father in him. Jesus' prayer was more than communication with another; it was communing at the deepest possible level with One from whom he was distinct but not separate. Jesus' oneness with the Father runs through the Johannine narrative of the

Last Supper. In the bit of dialogue that surfaces in chapter 14, Philip, slightly piqued by Jesus' talk about the Father whom — so he feels — they had never seen, suggests: "Lord, show us the Father and that will be enough for us" (14:8). Jesus' reply is quick and clear: "Whoever has seen me has seen the Father. . . . Do you not believe that I am in the Father and the Father is in me?" (14:9b–10a).

Prayer as Conversation:
An Analogy Sometimes Overliteralized

This danger — of overliteralizing the relationship with God that is the experience of prayer — lurks also in a very common way of conceiving *our* prayer, namely as talking with God. This is an analogy for understanding prayer that we borrow from our human experience of conversation with a friend. But it is possible to become too folksy about prayer and forget that in prayer we confront mystery. When we begin to think of prayer as "soft-chair" conversation with God or as a kind of cozy chat with a friend or (horrors!) with "the Person Upstairs," we must not forget that we are using an analogy. We must guard against "literalizing" the analogy. While it may be helpful to think of prayer as talking with God in the way we might talk with a friend, the analogy loses its usefulness, indeed it becomes positively misleading, if it moves us to believe that God is somehow separate from us: that we are here and God is there and we get in touch with Him from the outside. On the contrary, true prayer, especially contemplation, means going inside ourselves, going inside reality, going into "the temple" if you will, to find God and to find ourselves and all reality in God.

This notion of prayer as "going inside" is borne out by the rather curious etymology of the word "contemplation." A dictionary will tell you that contemplation means "to gaze attentively at something." The etymology takes us a big step further. At the heart of the word "contemplation" is the latin word *templum*, which means "temple." *Templum*, interestingly, is a diminutive of the word *tempus*. Generally *tempus* is translated as "time," yet its primary meaning is a "division or a section of time." Among the Romans the *templum* was a space in the sky or on the earth that was sectioned off or set apart for the augurs to read the omens. It was, therefore, a sacred spot marked off from other space, and generally in this spot the augurs would examine the entrails of birds. In other words, the temple was the place where certain sacred persons looked "inside animals, inside things," to find divine meanings and purposes.

Looking attentively at the "insides" of things might well be a way of describing contemplation. It is looking at ourselves, looking at reality, from the "inside." It is looking into the temple, where the "insides" of reality are to be found. If we go deeply enough into the "insides" of reality, we find that of themselves they are — nothing. They *are* only because at the very deepest level of reality we find a Source which is their Origin and the Ground in which they find their identity and their uniqueness. And that Source which is their Origin and Ground is God.

Distinct but Not Separate

Another way of putting what I am trying to say would be to state that God and I (as also the rest of reality) are not separate. We are distinct, for I am not God; but we cannot be separate, for apart from God I am nothing. To clarify this point, let us return to the analogy for prayer that we discussed earlier, namely, talking with a friend. Imagine such a conversation. You are talking with your friend. The two of you are together in the room in which you are meeting; there is you and there is your friend. Suppose that, after a bit of conversation, your friend leaves to keep another appointment. After her departure, there is only you. Where before there were two in the room, now there is only one present and that is you.

When we think of God and ourselves in the experience of prayer, we have to think quite differently. Thus it would be a misunderstanding to think that when I pray there are two namely, God and I. No, God and I equal not two, but one. For I cannot be separated from God, since God is the Ground in whom alone I find my being, my identity, my uniqueness. The equation of prayer, then, is: God plus me equals one, not two.

Once I appreciate this, there follows the (at first thought) shattering realization that I minus God equal zero. For when the Ground of my being is removed, I simply cease to be. It is, therefore, impossible for me to conceive of myself as apart from God. Apart from God, I simply do not exist. I am not there. But the experience after being "shattering" becomes positively exhilarating when I realize that the converse of this must also be true: namely, that if I do exist, I exist in God. Where I am, God is; or—more properly—I am where God is. There is no place else where I could be. This means that when I start to pray, I do not have "to place myself in the presence of God." For that is where I always am, whether I am always aware of it or not. The goal of prayer—I have already suggested this as the fundamental theme of this book—is to become aware that I am in God. Prayer is asking God: "May we experience the joy of life in your presence" (from the Alternate Prayer for the Seventeenth Sunday of Ordinary Time). Then we shall be able to say, in the words of Psalm 116: "I shall walk in the presence of the Lord in the land of the living" (v. 9).

The Illusion of God as "a Being"*

I also suggested earlier that one of the tasks of this book was to try to remove the "veils," the "illusions" that prevent us from being aware of God's presence. One of the illusions we must rid

*Some of this material appeared in modified form in "Thomas Merton and Freedom," *Cithara*, May 1981, pp. 25–26.

ourselves of is a tendency—probably left over from our former excessive preoccupation with an apologetics that "desperately" needed to "prove the existence of God"—to think of God as "a being" among other beings or as "an object" among other objects—a "being" or "object" whose existence can be discovered and demonstrated and whose "qualities" can be neatly described. This of course is not the true God at all; it is an idol, an illusion. We fail to appreciate the meaning of God, the Absolute One, unless we understand the Absolute "as neither existing nor not existing, but as being the ground of all that exists . . ." "It is not another 'existence' added to the existents grounded in it" (Merton, Holographic Journal, no. 28). He/She transcends them all and hence is not to be sought among them (see *The Hidden Ground of Love*, p. 450).

The true God, then, as compared to the illusory idol of a god who is *a being*, is the One who is beyond all beings. "God," Merton writes, "is the ALL, beyond all limits, beyond all definitions, beyond all human appreciation." "That which is ALL," he continues, "is no limited or individual thing. The ALL is no-thing, for if it were to be a single thing separated from all other things, it would not be ALL" (*Introductions East and West*, p. 44).

It is, therefore, a misunderstanding of the transcendence of God to conceive Him as "there" and creatures as "here." It is only in the order of logic that we can differentiate the transcendence of God from His immanence. God must not be divided: Once God wills to create, His transcendence necessarily flows into His immanence. The "Wholly Other" (the transcendent One) is inseparable from the "ALL" (the immanent One). It is precisely because God is *transcendent*, that is to say, not one in a series of beings, that He is *immanent*, namely, present in all things as the Source whence they come and the Ground in which they continue to be. He is in all and all exist because of Him and in Him.

A Text from Eckhart

In one of his notebooks (Holographic Journal, no. 43) dated 9 date of 9 October 1968, Merton quotes a remarkable passage from Master Eckhart, in which the renowned fourteenth-century Rhineland mystic, who often took delight in shocking his hearers, expresses in his own way what Merton means when he refers to God as the "ALL." "The Divine One," Eckhart says, "is a negation of negations and a denial of denials." He goes on to explain:

> Every creature contains a negative: a denial that it is the other. God contains the denial of denials. He is the One who denies of every other that it is anything but Himself.

What Eckhart is saying is that creatures are finite, that is to say, their being is limited. A particular creature is "this," not "that." It is the very limitation of their being that distinguishes them one from another. To say that a *horse* is a *horse* is to deny that it is a *house*. This is what Eckhart means when he says that every creature contains a negative: a denial that it is the other.

But God, he says, contains the denial of denials. God is not only "not this" and "not that"; He is at the same time a denial that He is "not this" and "not that." For "this" and "that," namely, all creatures that are, find their being, their identity and their uniqueness in Him. God is the *transcendent* One: He is not to be sought among creatures, for God is neither "this" nor "that." At the same time God is the *immanent* One: He must be a denial that He is neither "this" nor "that," because God is the Source and Ground of all that is. Every "this" and "that" finds its reality in Him.

The "Knowing" Heart

Yet we must be aware of the inadequacy of all human efforts to describe God. We must beware, therefore, lest in trying to describe Him, we turn the living God into a philosopher's abstraction. He who is not "this" and not "that," yet who is ALL, cannot be grasped by a perception of the mind: He eludes all our efforts to contain Him within our feeble reasoning. Rather the "ALL" is to be responded to with our hearts. "The heart only," Merton writes, "is capable of knowing God" (Holographic Journal, no. 18). In the context of this statement, he quotes a saying of Allah attributed to the prophet Muhammad:

My earth and heaven cannot contain me,
But the heart of my believing servant contains me.

The human heart, Merton comments, is the only place strong enough to bear the divine secret: the secret of who He is.

"Prayer of the Desert"

By now it is probably clear to the reader that when I speak of prayer, I especially have in mind that quiet, sometimes wordless prayer in which we seek to deepen our awareness of God's presence in our lives and in our world. This simple, humble prayer that seeks just to *be* in conscious awareness of God may be called "the prayer of awareness." Another name for this type of prayer that has become very popular is "centering prayer." It might also be called "the prayer of the desert," because in Scripture the desert appears as the privileged place where God manifests His presence to His people. But, whatever we call it, we all need it, not because we may happen to be Christians, but simply because we are human persons who need to be awakened continually and ever more fully to the fact that we are in God.

"Prayer of the Choir"

Besides this "prayer of the desert" there is another type of prayer that I would like to call the "prayer of the choir." I suggest this name not because it is prayer that we sing (although we do sing

it at times), but because what a choir is supposed to do expresses most clearly what this kind of prayer ought to be.

What is it that a choir does in song? First and foremost, it
praises God and offers thanksgiving to Him. Praise and
thanksgiving say what Christians do when they gather on the
Lord's Day for the Eucharist. For Eucharist means at once
praise and thanks. The choir also expresses in its song a sense
of repentance and the need for reconciliation in the community. In the Sacred Scriptures the human desire to praise and
thank God for all that He does for His people vies for primacy
of place with the human need to seek the divine forgiveness in a
people all too conscious of their infidelities to a gracious Lord.
It is because they experience themselves as sinful that there is
this strong impulse to seek reconciliation with God; it is because they experience their dependence as creatures that they
feel constrained to move in yet another direction in prayer,
namely, to petitioning God for help in other areas of their lives.
In fact, intercessory prayer has always played a dominant role
in the human approach to God. Praise, thanksgiving, repentance, and intercession — these are the characteristic elements
of the "prayer of the choir." Whether or not we are ever a part of
a choir, these sentiments of the "prayer of the choir" must burst
forth from our hearts in prayer, whether we are praying with
Scripture or saying our own vocal prayers or the prayers of
liturgy.

Reading

In this chapter devoted to a general understanding of prayer, I
would be remiss if I failed to include what Christian tradition
has normally seen as the necessary preparation for and accompaniment of prayer, namely, *lectio divina*, or the reading of "sacred books." Admittedly "sacred book" is a clumsy, perhaps
even misleading, term. No book as mere printed material can
be called "sacred." When I speak of "sacred books" I mean to

include writings that are especially intended to mediate God's Word to us. Primacy and pride of place among such works must be given to the sacred books of the Old and New Testaments that enshrine a never-to-be-repeated experience and, because they do, mediate the Word of God in a unique way. Because Christians believe this, there is a "canon" of Sacred Scriptures, and the books listed in this canon enjoy special authority. Second in authority and importance as "sacred books" would be the writings of the Fathers of the Church whose close proximity to, and continuity with, the writings of Sacred Scripture give them a special claim to a hearing from those who seek to listen to the Word of God.

The Fathers of the Church

Who are the Fathers of the Church? If a textbook definition will satisfy, they are the ecclesiastical writers of Christian antiquity whose teaching was orthodox, whose lives were holy and who, therefore, have been approved, officially or unofficially, by the Church as witnesses to its faith. Perhaps it is not enough to say they were "orthodox," for in many ways it was their writings that determined what orthodoxy really was. Perhaps one way of describing them is that they were "theologians," but their theology was not so much speculation about Christian faith as it was reflection on what it meant to live as a Christian and to be moved to action by the Sacred Scriptures.

There is no general agreement as to when the period of the Fathers comes to an end. Those nearest to the Apostolic Age are called the ante-Nicene Fathers and would include people like Ignatius of Antioch, Polycarp, Clement, Irenaeus, etc. The "Golden Age" of the Fathers is that period that coincides, more or less, with the first four great Councils of the Church: Nicaea (325), Constantinople (381), Ephesus (431), and Chalcedon (451). There are big names here and only a few need be mentioned by way of illustration: Athanasius, Cyril of

Alexandria, Evagrius Ponticus, the three Cappadocians (Basil of Caesarea, Gregory of Nazianzus, and Gregory of Nyssa), also Cyril of Jerusalem, John Chrysostom, Ambrose, Jerome, and (surely one of the giants) Augustine of Hippo. Some would close the Patristic Age with John Damascene (d. c. 750) in the East and with Isidore of Seville (d. 636) in the West. Clearly this is quite arbitrary; indeed the Cistercians like to think of St. Bernard who died in 1153 as "the last of the Fathers."

Other Christian Writers

Besides the Scriptures and the Fathers, I would like to include among "sacred books" a much more ambiguously definable listing, namely, the works of those Christian writers who through the ages appear as faithful purveyors of the tradition of faith and insightful readers of the "signs of the times." I would not want to hazard a list, as it would likely be highly personal, though if I were pressed to offer a name or two, I would venture the names of John Henry Newman of the last century and Thomas Merton of the present one.

Lectio or reading is, as I have already suggested, a preparation for and an accompaniment of prayer. Indeed, *lectio* and reflection on it (*meditatio*) very often lead directly into prayer. So true is this, that the phrase *lectio divina* is often used as an abbreviated way of describing a whole way of prayer that involves four steps or four rungs on a ladder: reading, meditation, prayer, and contemplation.

This way of prayer (I do not want to call it a "method," since it really involves no hard-and-fast rules) has a long history in Christian spirituality. While the fundamentals of these four steps are found in the very early tradition of the Church, they have been given classical expression in a work by Guigo II, the ninth prior of the Grand Chartreuse, the motherhouse of the Carthusian Order. He sets forth this tradition in the literary form of a letter called *Scala Claustralium* (*The Ladder of Monks*) addressed to his friend, Brother Gervase. Guigo died in 1188. The subsequent tradition knew his work very well. Influential as it was, it was at different times ascribed to St. Augustine, to St. Bernard, and to others. (In fact, the Latin text of Guigo is found in Migne's *Patrologia Latina* among the works of St. Augustine — though there is a forenote by the editor indicating that it actually does belong to Guigo. The work has been known by other names; there is the delightful title: "The Ladder to Paradise," and one less grandiose: "A Treatise on How to Pray.") The *Ladder* became a favorite work in the late Middle Ages not only for monks but for lay people as well. St. John of the Cross was well acquainted with this tradition of prayer. He writes in *Maxims and Counsels*:

> Seek in reading and you will find in meditation;
> knock in prayer and it will be opened to you in contemplation.

And, earlier than John of the Cross, the author of *The Cloud of Unknowing* expressed his appreciation of the same wisdom when he spoke of the place of reading, thinking, and praying on the way to contemplation.

Guigo's *Ladder*

Guigo tells his friend, Brother Gervase, that he is sending him his thoughts about different kinds of spiritual exercise that ought to be carried out by a person committed to living a spiritual life. He asks Gervase to pass judgment on his thoughts and to correct them if need be. Guigo tells Gervase that he is well qualified to make such an evaluation, because "you have come to know more about these matters by your experience than I have by theorizing about them." The thoughts that came to Guigo — all of a sudden, as he tells us, while he was working in the fields — are about the four rungs of the ladder by which we are lifted up to heaven. The "ladder" image, a familiar one in mystical writings, is taken from the biblical story of Genesis 28:10–19 in which Jacob sees a staircase or a ladder resting on the ground with its top reaching to the heavens. Guigo makes clear that, though the ladder has only four rungs, it is, like Jacob's, an immense and wondrous ladder, since one end of it rests on the earth while its topmost part pierces the clouds and reaches through them to attain the very secrets of heaven.

The four rungs of the "ladder" that came to Guigo's mind are the four ways in which a person can exercise himself/herself spiritually. It should be noted that Guigo uses the word "exercise" in the singular. He is not speaking primarily about a series of exercises for some special time, but rather about the kind of exercising that is regularly necessary for the good of the spirit, as walking, running, jogging, etc., are valuable exercises one ought to engage in regularly for the good of the body. The kinds of exercise Guigo speaks of are: reading, meditation, prayer, and contemplation. Here is his initial description of them:

> *Reading* is a careful study of the Scriptures, in which the person's whole attention is engaged.
>
> *Meditation* is an action of the mind probing the Scriptures and seeking with reason's help to know the truth hidden therein.
>
> *Prayer* is the intent turning of the heart to God asking Him to rid us of evil and obtain for us what is good.
>
> *Contemplation* is the devout lifting of the mind to God, in such a way that it transcends itself and comes to taste the joys of an everlasting sweetness. (Migne, *P.L.* 40 998, my translation)

Guigo offers a simple example to clarify what he means by these four rungs of the ladder of spiritual exercise. He chooses a text from Matthew's Gospel (5:8): "Blessed are the pure in heart, for they shall see God." This is a short text, he says, but full of sweetness. He likens it to a grape someone might put in his mouth. The person says: There is something good here. I must try to understand what this "purity of heart" is, because those who possess it are called blessed and are rewarded with the vision of God. Moreover, it is also praised in other places in Scripture.

"So," and I quote Guigo, "wishing to have a fuller understanding of this, the soul begins to bite and chew upon this grape [that is, the text from Matthew's Gospel], as though putting it in a wine press, while it stirs up its powers of reasoning to ask what this precious purity may be and how it may be had" (Image translation, p. 83). Meditation goes to the heart of the matter, examining each point thoroughly. It notes carefully that the text does not refer simply to being pure in body, but pure in the heart. It recalls other references in Scripture. Psalm 24, for instance, asks: "Who shall climb the mountain of the Lord, and who shall stand in His holy place?" And the answer is: "The one whose hands are guiltless and *whose heart is pure.*" Meditation also remembers that the psalmist prays: "Create a *clean heart* in me, God."

Meditation moves one to long for this purity in order to experience what it leads to: seeing God, beholding His Face. Thus meditation leads to prayer: the prayer of longing, desire, and praise, and eventually it leads to the sweetness that comes with seeing God.

Guigo goes on to say: "Do you see how much juice has come from one little grape" (then he switches his metaphor), "how great a fire has been kindled from a spark" (and yet another switch), "how this small piece of metal, 'Blessed are the pure in heart, for they shall see God,' has acquired a new dimension by being hammered out on the anvil of meditation? (Image translation, pp. 84–85).

Guigo then proceeds to discuss each of the four steps separately. It will suffice here to quote the summary he gives:

Reading comes first as a kind of foundation: it gives us the subject matter we need to reflect on and then sends us (*mittit nos*) to meditation.

Meditation inquires assiduously for what we should be seeking: it digs deeply, as it were, and uncovers the hidden treasure so that we can see it. But since it cannot of itself attain to that treasure, it sends us (*mittit nos*) to prayer.

Prayer, which lifts us up to God with all its might, begs for the wondrous treasure which is nothing other than the sweetness of contemplation.

Contemplation when it comes (*adveniens*) rewards the labors of the other three endeavors, as it inebriates the soul and slakes its thirst with the dew of heavenly sweetness. (Op. cit., 1002, my translation)

Finally, he gives a quick summary:

Reading is an exercise of our outer senses;
Meditation of our inner understanding.
Prayer has to do with desire;
Contemplation goes beyond all sense and thought. (Ibid.)

Concluding Observations

I should like to conclude this chapter by making three observations. First of all, it is essential to the main thrust of this book that I point out how, in the very long tradition that Guigo draws on and that remained for a long time the accepted tradition, there is never any thought of confusing meditation with contemplation. In post-Reformation spirituality, unhappily, this has not always been true. In fact, today the two terms are often used interchangeably. This represents an unfortunate turn of events and tends to impoverish our understanding of prayer and especially of the proper meaning of contemplation.

The second observation I wish to make may well be already clear to the reader. She/he may have noted by now that the two kinds of prayer discussed in this chapter find their counterparts in two of the rungs of Guigo's ladder. What Guigo calls *oratio* or "prayer" corresponds to what I have referred to as "the prayer of the choir"; and "the prayer of the desert" is nothing other than Guigo's "contemplation." Hopefully both these observations and their significance will become clearer as we move further into the book.

The third observation I want to propose to the reader is the need for support in one's effort to make *lectio divina* and its "concomitants" a regular reality in one's life. We cannot ignore the fact that we live in a cultural milieu that consistently ignores the needs of the spirit. I recommend the formation of prayer groups of a dozen people or so who meet regularly for a simple program in which they spend perhaps an hour and a half climbing together the four rungs of Guigo's ladder. I am a member of such a group that comes together once each month. At the meeting the Gospel for the coming Sunday's liturgy is read aloud (and slowly) by the group in unison; then it is read silently by each person in the group, after which there is a third reading—aloud and by the whole group. The intent is simple: to let the words of the Gospel seep into our minds and hearts.

Following the reading (the *lectio*), there is a period of reflection (*meditatio*): each person has the opportunity to say what he or she wishes, with no comments from the others. Once each person has been allowed her/his say, time is given for reflection and application from any one in the group. Following the reflection, some time is allotted for prayer (*oratio*). Members of the group will express, in short prayer, their thanks, praise, desire for reconciliation, their own needs and those of the Church and the world. At the end of the prayer period, the group sits in silent, wordless prayer (*contemplatio*) for a half hour, seeking to experience the joy of life lived consciously in God's presence. The silence that sometimes comes during the session and the silence that concludes it were initially uncomfortable for some. But as time has gone on, many have said that they feel, almost unaccountably, drawn more and more to this silence. In spite of the many distractions that often come, the silence seems a response to a need more and more deeply experienced in the inner recesses of their being.

A final word of caution. I would not want to give the impression that I am speaking of a "method or formula of prayer" that should be rigidly adhered to. Guigo's ladder, at least as I interpret it, is not so much a formula as a simple way of moving from words to wordlessness. This "movement" may take place at a single session or it may be extended over a longer or shorter period of time. It all depends on what best suits the individual or the group that may be praying together. In fact, it may well happen that this kind of progression from one rung to the next may not meet the needs of an individual or a group at a particular time. There might well be times when a person or a group would be quite content with reading mingled with prayer, or times when their desire would be to move immediately beyond words into wordless prayer. What matters is not a formula but that we become aware of God's presence in our lives. Whatever way of praying helps us to that awareness is right for us.

3

The First Rung
of Guigo's Ladder: *Lectio*

This chapter will attempt to discuss in more detail the first rung on the prayer-ladder described by Guigo and referred to briefly at the end of the last chapter. It should be clear that there is a bit of artificiality in discussing these steps one by one, for in the actual practice of prayer they are not necessarily separated. One does not read without some reflection (meditation) on what is read. Reading easily moves into prayer and can find its rest in contemplation. Yet it is still true that reading is not identical with meditation or prayer or contemplation. It is possible therefore to *think and talk* about each of the rungs of the ladder separately. I want to proceed, then, to discuss *lectio divina*.

The Art of Reading
Before discussing the reading of God's Word, it will be helpful to reflect briefly on the role that reading in general plays in human life. Before we talk about the word-encounter that *lectio divina* makes possible between God and us, we should take a quick glance at a marvelous fact that we so readily take for granted, namely, the power that reading gives us of transcending space and time and encountering the knowledge and wisdom of the ages. Reading enables us to participate in the

thought-life that belongs to our culture, past and present; it makes us "citizens" of other countries and thoughtful observers of other ages. It offers us an instrument for interpreting our experience; it makes possible the vicarious experience of what we could never know firsthand. Most of all perhaps, reading gives us an entry into the minds of people we have never met and never will, save through the written word. We meet the other through the powerful, though fragile, medium of words.

Words are *powerful*: they can rend hearts or mend them, open minds or shatter them, they can foment revolution or produce social change through nonviolence. Yet words are also *fragile*: they can be misread, misunderstood, misinterpreted. They can be abused and turned to the service of causes they were never intended to promote. They can be used to coerce, when they were intended to free. They can be received with complacency, when their purpose was to challenge. They can be banal or they can reach the very roots of human joy and anguish.

Reading — which puts words to work in all their power and fragility — is one of the great dignities that men and women possess: the dignity of sharing with another or with others their minds, their hearts, their very persons. Reading enables us, through communication with others, to grow in knowledge and wisdom, both human and divine. Good reading is critical reading; it enables us to reach beneath the surface meaning of words to the deeper intentions the writer wishes to convey. We may even discover hidden implications that do indeed emerge from the text, even though they may not have been in the author's conscious intent when he/she wrote.

Most religions have prized the power of the word and therefore reading has always had a special place in the lives of their adherents. It is not surprising, then, to find that *lectio divina*, as a Christian exercise, boasts a long history. The expression of course means, literally, "divine reading" or, perhaps better, reading about God and the things of God.

Foundations in Judaism

Lectio divina has its roots in Judaism, especially in the exilic period, when Israel had no sacrifice to offer and no temple in which to offer it. At this point in their history — it would be the sixth century B.C. — the Word of God in their Sacred Scriptures became the staple of their worship. It was in order to have a place to hear the Law and the Prophets and to be instructed about them that a new institution came into existence in the life of Israel: namely, the synagogue. The synagogue should not be confused with the temple. The temple was the place for sacrifices to God, whereas the synagogue was the place for public *lectio divina*, the reading and hearing of the Word of God within the assembly of God's people. And after the destruction of Jerusalem in A.D. 70, when there no longer was a temple in which to offer sacrifice, it was Jewish *lectio divina*, the reading of the Word of God, that enabled Israel to survive as a religion and as a nation. Throughout what became a tragic history, deeply marked by persecution, it has continued to survive on the Word of God.

Lectio Divina in the Early Church

The reading of the Scriptures became an important part of the life of the early Church. (At first of course it was only the Hebrew Scriptures — for it was mostly the post-apostolic generation that began the writing of the New Testament Scriptures; and quite a number of generations passed before the full canon received ecclesial approval.) For we know that the Church, when it finally separated once and for all from Judaism (about A.D. 85), took over the reading (*lectio*) service of the synagogue, which became the first part of the Christian liturgy and has remained so even till today. What we now call the "Liturgy of the Word" could well be described as a public *lectio divina*.

I should make it clear that the phrase *lectio divina* was not used to designate the public reading of the Scriptures, but rather the reading of them in private by individuals. This private reading of the Scriptures was the age-old habit of the rabbis. Sometimes they did it in twos; and according to an ancient rabbinic saying, when two pious Jews read the Torah together the *Shekinah* (the Holy Presence) of God overshadowed them. Indeed, so highly was this sacred reading extolled that there were some who made the rather extravagant claim that God Himself took time each day to read the Torah. This would certainly be *lectio divina* in the fullest sense of the word!

Christians followed not only the practice of public reading of Scripture that existed in Judaism, they also took over the custom of regular reading of the Word of God in private. It will not serve our purpose here to go into a great deal of historical detail as to how *lectio divina* developed in the early centuries of the Christian Church. There is evidence of its existence certainly at the end of the second and the beginning of the third century. A principal center was the flourishing Church in Alexandria, where Origen (185–254) outlined the basic practice of the reading of Scripture. For him the source and foundation of all true knowledge is to be sought in the reading of and the meditating on Scripture; but he was very clear that it is not human acumen but God's grace that brings understanding of God's Word—grace that at times may be experienced suddenly and unexpectedly.

Lectio divina continued to evolve especially among the monks in the third and fourth centuries. St. Basil, St. Pachomius, and St. Jerome built on the ideas of Origen. Jerome (342–420), who produced the Latin translation of the Scriptures that became the Church's official version (the Vulgate) for centuries, summed up the thinking of the early monastic tradition when he said in his *Commentary on the Prophet Isaiah*:

> One who does not know the scriptures
> does not know the power and wisdom of God;
> Ignorance of the Scriptures is ignorance of Christ.

Jerome writes about the importance of memorizing the Scriptures and getting its words into the heart. St. Pachomius (290–346), the founder of cenobitic monasticism in Egypt, would not tolerate illiteracy among his monks. If they wanted to be monks they had to learn to read. Their ability to do *lectio divina* was that important to him. And it was St. Basil (330–379), whose monastic "Rule" is followed by many monasteries in the Eastern Church, who speaks of the importance of *savoring* the texts of Scripture. This was to become in the Middle Ages a favorite image of what it meant to read the Scriptures.

Lectio Divina in the Rule of St. Benedict

The monastic Rule that predominated in the West, the *Rule of St. Benedict* (c. 480–c. 550) gives a prominent place to *lectio divina*. Chapter 48 of the *Rule* states:

> Idleness is an enemy of the soul. Therefore the brothers should be occupied according to schedule in either manual labor or holy reading.

Holy reading is, of course, *lectio divina*. The same chapter of the *Rule* then goes on to specify how the hours of the day are to be distributed, around the Divine Office, for manual labor and holy reading. The year is divided into three different periods according to the amount of daylight. At the beginning of each period, each monk is to be given a book from the library, which he should read carefully from cover to cover.

If we are to appreciate fully the role that *lectio divina* played in the monastic tradition, we need to understand what reading (*legere*) meant to St. Benedict, as well as for the ages before him and the ages that followed him. Today we read principally with the eyes. In antiquity and in the Middle Ages, people read with the lips as well as with the eyes: not only seeing with their eyes what was on the page, but also hearing with their ears the sounds that the words on the page represented. Reading thus meant not only seeing the words on the pages, it also meant hearing the "voices of the pages." *Legere*, in other words, was what Dom LeClercq calls "acoustical reading." *Legere* was also *audire*. Reading included hearing. (One wonders whether the obligation of moving the lips in the reading of the Divine Office, which has been understood as the proper way on the part of those in Holy Orders of fulfilling the obligation of "saying the Office," is a remnant of this age-old practice.)

No doubt silent reading was not unknown. But its infrequency as a way of reading is indicated by the fact that when it is being referred to, it is described as such. Thus *tacite legere* or *legere sibi* designate something out of the ordinary, something different from *clara lectio*. Normally, when *legere* or *lectio* are used without any qualification, they refer to an activity that, like chanting or writing, involves the whole person. Dom Jean Leclercq — to whom I am indebted for much of this information — says that physicians of ancient times used to recommend reading to their patients as a physical exercise on an equal level with walking, running, or ball-playing (see Jean Leclercq, *The Love of Learning and the Desire for God* [New York: Fordham University Press, 1961], p. 19).

It is worthy of note that in chapter 48 of the *Rule of St. Benedict*, to which I referred earlier, the monks are directed to rest (in bed) after dinner. "However," the *Rule* says, "should anyone desire to read, he should do so without disturbing his brothers." This is a clear indication that the normal way of reading would be disturbing. The reason is that it would be done aloud; it would be words spoken as well as seen.

An Important Difference

This brief excursus on the history and character of *lectio divina* was intended simply to enable us to understand more clearly how this spiritual exercise has come down to us and, further, to help us see how it can become a reality in the life of a twentieth-century Christian. In an age wherein books are available in huge numbers, it is important to understand how *lectio divina* differs from simple *lectio*. Whereas *lectio* aims at answering questions and satisfying the curiosity of the mind, *lectio divina* aims more at challenging the heart. While it would be wrong to think of *lectio divina* as anti-intellectual, it would be equally incorrect to think that its purpose is simply to communicate knowledge or information. Even though such communication does take place, in varying degrees, the final goal of *lectio divina* is to initiate and deepen the conversion process in the one who reads. It seeks to draw the reader ever more fully into union with Jesus Christ, who is the perfect image of God. It is reading mingled with prayer and contact with God.

A Biblical Image from Isaiah

We can learn from the Bible itself the importance of Holy Scripture and the purpose it is intended to accomplish. There is a moving — and probably very familiar — passage in Second Isaiah that expresses in beautiful imagery what reading the Word of God and listening to it meant in the community of Israel. (And it is worth noting that Second Isaiah would probably come from the period of the exile when the Israelites, living in Babylon, had no temple; they had only their Scriptures.) This passage would also have had deep meaning for the Christian community, as the reading of the Holy Scriptures continued to play a role of paramount importance in Christian life. The passage from Second Isaiah reads:

> Just as from the heavens
>   the rain and snow come down
> And do not return there
>   till they have watered the earth,
>   making it fertile and fruitful
>   giving seed to him who sows
>   and bread to him who eats,

So shall my Word be
   that goes forth from my mouth;
It shall not return to me void
   but shall do my will
   achieving the end for which I sent it. (55:10-11)

Reflection on this text can help us to understand what *lectio divina* meant to the early Christians and to the rabbis before them. The text speaks of God's Word as "rain" or "snow." When we reflect on the first image of rain, we may perhaps think of two different types of rain. There is the *brief rain* that covers the surface of the ground, but without really penetrating the ground. This rain may settle the dust, but it does little to make the ground fertile and fruitful.

But there is another kind of rain: the *long, gentle rain* — what in Ireland is called the "soft" rain. This not only covers the surface, it also gets beneath that surface. It reaches deep down into the soil. If this kind of rain persists for a reasonable length of time, the ground becomes saturated; it is full of water; it becomes fertile and fruitful.

We shall derive little benefit from a quick, cursory reading of Scripture that skims over the words and lets them remain on the surface of our lives instead of reaching down deeply into the soil of our hearts. What is important is that, through *repeated, continuous, unhurried* reading, we allow our whole persons to be saturated, filled to overflowing, with the Word of God. We do not even, initially at least, have to react to it. Instead we should simply let the Word happen to us. Let it be the soft, gentle, ongoing rain that comes into our lives and by its power makes them fertile and fruitful.

Our passage also likens the Word of God to snow. There is a difference between rain and snow in terms of what they do to the ground. The rain tends to saturate the ground gradually, gently, — but rather swiftly. The snow, however, falls generally on ground that has become hard and frozen. It may remain on the surface for a long time. Only gradually does the snow melt and then begin to penetrate into the depths of the soil. During winter we have to be patient, waiting for the ground to thaw, to warm up, so that the snow can melt and eventually saturate the soil.

Sometimes the Word of God penetrates our hearts quickly — like the gentle, soft rains. Sometimes our hearts may be harder and, just as it takes time for the snow to penetrate the frozen ground, so it takes time and patience for the Word to dig its roots into our sometimes hardened hearts. The Word of God has to unfreeze and warm our hearts before it can produce lasting fruit in them.

In an age of speed reading and multitudinous distractions, we have to learn to read slowly and with careful attention. We have to deal gently and lovingly with the words that enshrine the Word. If *lectio divina* is to be an effective instrument of conversion in our lives, we have to read the words of Holy Scripture over and over again till they pierce us through. They have to be captured in our memory so that they can continually return to our minds. The sermons of many of the Fathers of the Church seem almost like *catenae* of texts from Sacred Scripture strung together. This is not an attempt on the part of the Fathers to impress us with their knowledge of the Scriptures; rather the words of Scripture were so much intertwined with the vocabulary of words in their minds and with the affections of their hearts that they quite spontaneously emerge in what they say and write. I am reminded of a young student who came to a rabbi and asked what he needed to do to become a teacher of the Scriptures himself. The rabbi asked him: "What have you done so far?" "I have gone through the Torah," he replied. "Good," said the rabbi, "but has the Torah gone through you?" It is one thing to go through the Scriptures, another to let them take possession of our minds and hearts. This is the intent of *lectio divina*.

Some Suggestions about *Lectio Divina*

For those who would like to use *lectio divina* as a stage on the way to contemplation (or as a "rung" on the "ladder," to keep us in the context of Guigo's analogy), I would offer the following brief suggestions:

1. There should be a regular, ideally daily, reading of the Holy Scriptures. One can be most free in the choice of what to read. It could be the reading or readings for the current day's liturgy, or one might want to spend the whole week on the readings for the following Sunday as, among other things, a way of preparing for a fitting celebration of the Lord's Day. Or one might want to choose a particular book of the Bible and read it through from beginning to end.

2. There is need to ready our hearts and minds for listening to the Word of God. If we come to *lectio* in a state of overstimulation — with ideas, plans, concerns, anxieties — our minds and hearts will find it difficult, if not impossible, to be receptive. There is so much else happening inside us that the "Word" cannot "happen."

Over the past few years I have become initiated into, and become addicted to, computers and word-processing. While I don't know much about the technology involved, there is one simple fact I learned very early: you cannot simply take a "floppy disk" out of a box, put it into your computer, and expect it to receive the data you send it. First of all, it has to "initialized" or "formatted" so that its grooves are able to receive what you send it. Like the disks, our minds and hearts have to be "initialized" or "formatted" so that we may be able to receive the Word of God that speaks to us through the words of the text. There is, however, a correction that must be made in the analogy. The disk has to move from being totally blank to becoming receptive. We, on the other hand, do not generally approach *lectio* with minds that are blank and unoccupied. On the contrary, we are most likely to be in a situation wherein we are overwhelmed with all sorts of distractions and will need to clear out our minds, to empty them, in order to be receptive to the Word and its call.

My experience with word-processing suggests yet another analogy that may be helpful in understanding what we must do in the "pre-*lectio*" period. When on a particular occasion you begin to use a disk, there may already be a number of documents that you have previously filed on it. If you give the proper signal, you can delete one or a number of these documents. In fact, it is possible to delete all of them if you wish. Then you will have a disk perfectly free to receive whatever new material you send it.

One of the frustrations one can encounter in doing word-processing is overloading a disk by mistake. You may type data into your computer, give the signal for it to be transferred to the disk, only to have the computer tell you: "Sorry, the disk is already full." There may be times when we shall have to look at the documents that are filed in our mind-heart computer and — at least for the time of prayer — we may have to delete some or all of them, if we are really in earnest about receiving God's Word. But once again the analogy needs correction. When you have deleted something from the disk, it is gone beyond recall: it cannot be retrieved. The tasks, concerns, and anxieties that occupy us may be such that they cannot be deleted once and for all. There may be situations in our lives that we have no right to ignore and must deal with responsibly. Yet deleting them from our minds and hearts for a brief period of time each day during our prayer may enable us to approach them with fresh insight. It may also help us to put them in better perspective in the total context of our lives so that they do not overwhelm or cripple us.

3. Though not strictly necessary, try to read the text aloud so that you hear the words as well as see them.

4. Read a particular text a number of times, so that it can become part of you and fixed to some degree in the memory. I mentioned earlier that St. Pachomius insisted on the importance of the reading of Scripture for his monks. He is said to

have known the whole Bible by heart and to have expected that, at the very least, his monks would gradually commit to memory the Psalms and the New Testament. We tend to rely too much on the everpresent availability of the printed word; we need to have more of the Scriptures imprinted on our memories.

5. Read slowly. Do not hesitate to pause during reading. Nothing is more harmful to fruitful prayer than haste. There is no need for rushing. We don't have to "cover a lot of ground."

6. At the *lectio* stage, be attentive to the words of the sacred text but not reflective about them. Just let the Word of God happen to you. Let it come like the gentle rain and softly soak into your heart. This is not the time for analyzing the text and applying it to your life; that will come later in the stage of meditation. At this stage it is enough to let the Word come and to absorb it — almost like a blotter. For the time being you must leave the Word to itself. Let it accomplish its own purposes, achieving the end for which God sent it.

7. When we read the Scriptures, some word or phrase may emerge from our reading that glows with a meaning it never had for us before. Such a word or phrase becomes a "word of salvation" for you. You may want to repeat it a number of times during the day. You may even want, on occasion, to share it with a friend. In this connection, I would like to relate an experience I had recently in editing the first volume of the Merton letters (*The Hidden Ground of Love*). I was translating (from the French) a letter he had written to Archimandrite Sophrony, a monk of the Orthodox Church living in England. At first, I was puzzled by a sentence that said: "Dites moi un petit mot, une 'parole de salut,' cher Père." ("My dear Father, give me a brief word, 'a word of salvation.'") Then I realized that Merton was following a very ancient monastic custom, which would be especially dear to monks from the East: the custom of asking a spiritual master to give one "a word of salvation" that one could savor. It would have special meaning

because it was the gift of a master. Would this, I am presuming to ask, perhaps be a custom worth reviving, on a limited scale, among a group that has a common interest in prayer, especially a group that comes together regularly to pray? Without claiming to be "spiritual masters," we could yet exchange with one another a word or phrase that has touched our minds and hearts. We might even, on occasion and as a sign of our solidarity in the Lord, make the request of one another: "Give me a word of salvation."

4

The Second Rung: *Meditatio*

This chapter will deal with the second rung of the ladder of spiritual discipline that leads to Christian perfection, namely, meditation. *Meditatio* and *lectio divina* are very closely related, yet it would be a mistake to identify them. One way perhaps of expressing the difference between them is to say that *lectio divina* is more passive than *meditatio*. I must say, though, that I am not totally comfortable in using the word "passive" to describe *lectio divina*: I would certainly want to exclude some of the dictionary synonyms. Thus by "passive" I do not mean "indifferent" or "uninvolved," much less "lifeless" or "unresponsive." I use the word in the very literal sense of "being acted upon." As I have suggested in chapter 3, *lectio divina* means "letting the Word of God happen" to me. I use my lips as well as my eyes so that the Word is allowed to seep into my whole personality system, reaching my memory and my heart.

Meditation, on the other hand, is more active. Where *lectio* "receives," *meditatio* "reacts." It enters into dialogue with the Word to discover its meaning. The Latin word *meditari* means in a general way "to think." It is thus similar to the Latin *cogitare* and *considerare*, but while these tend to refer to a mental activity that remains primarily in the mind, *meditari* implies thinking that has a definite relationship to the moral order. It suggests thinking about something with the intention of doing what the thinking prompts one to do. It is thinking ordered to practice.

In meditation I appropriate a text so that the text becomes my own and is fixed in my heart as an inner principle of action. This appropriation of the Word takes place in the context of faith. I *believe* that it is the Word of God that has entered my heart. The stronger my faith is, the deeper God's Word is able to penetrate my being. The more open my heart, the more charged with the dynamic power of the Holy Spirit are the words I bring into that heart.

Perhaps a simple example will clarify the difference between *lectio* and *meditatio* and at the same time show the almost inseparable link between them. Suppose you are upset about the world situation: the threat of nuclear annihilation, the accelerating arms race. One day you meet a friend whom you have always respected but haven't seen for a long time. She tells you that she has come to believe that the only way to peace in the world is *satyagraha*, or nonviolence. You are sceptical, since you have always taken for granted that a strong military defense was the most effective deterrence to war. But because you respect your friend you want to hear what she has to say. You are open to her position. You let yourself by led by her. You are receptive: you let her views on nonviolence "happen" to you. You may have several talks. What she says enters your mind. You reflect on it, analyze it. Perhaps it eventually enters into your heart and takes hold of you. You may at last become convinced as your friend is that nonviolence is the only way to peace. You cannot rest with this conviction. You feel yourself obligated to act on it.

Lectio divina resembles your receptivity to your friend's views on nonviolence, whereas *meditatio* is your thinking and analysis, your arrival at conviction and the imperative you experience that you must do something to implement that conviction. If you were already somewhat favorably disposed toward nonviolence, your desire for active engagement in the peace movement would probably be that much stronger after talking with your friend. The faith and trust you have in your friend will furnish the context in which your dialogue and final acceptance take place. The more you trust your friend, the more likely are you to be open to receive and act upon the word she speaks to you.

Lectio and *Meditatio* — Closely Related

It is easy, then, to see that while they differ in a very fundamental way, there is a close connection, indeed almost an inseparable link, between *lectio* and *meditatio*. For the text that one fixes in the memory so as to have it become a principle of action in one's life is the text that you let "happen" to you in *reading*. Like the gentle rain, the text seeps through till it reaches our hearts and moves us to act. So closely linked are *lectio* and *meditatio* that in many instances they amount to the "passive" and "active" side of what is the same experience. For you do not meditate on an abstraction, you meditate on a text — a text that is read and heard. It is helpful in this connection to look at Psalm 37, verse 30. In the New American Bible, it reads: "The mouth of the just one *tells* of wisdom." Yet, in the Latin Vulgate, the verse is: "Os justi *meditabitur* sapientiam." "Telling" (that is, reading and hearing) and "meditating" are used interchangeably.

I do not want to belabor this point, but I need to make clear that for the ancients "to meditate" is to "put into the heart" a text that has been read. "Heart" in this context is to be given the fullest possible meaning. It means "the whole of one's being." It means the eyes that see the text, the mouth that pronounces it, the ears that hear it, the memory that fixes it within itself, the intelligence that grasps its meaning and the will that desires to respond to the text and put its demands into practice.

Meditation, then, is actively reflecting on a text, analyzing it, digging into it, learning what it means in your life. It may be accompanied (or preceded) by study. But it differs from study. For studying the text simply answers questions about its meaning, whereas meditation looks for the practical response that the text calls for. Study that elucidates the text can be helpful for fruitful meditation; it cannot, however, substitute for it. Each has a role — though a different one — to play in our lives. Study can stop when the mind is satisfied; meditation demands that study be put into action. Whereas study may be seen as reaction to concepts, meditation is response to meaning.

Meditation helps us to "see" the things of faith with an experiential grasp that goes beyond faith and grasps the inner meaning and relevance of the things we believe. Thus, it enables us to build a meaningful interior world of our own that empowers us to respond to the external circumstances of life with a consistency and a creativity that arise from continuous, ongoing exposure to God's Word, and also with a confidence that comes, not from ourselves, but from a growing docility to God's Spirit whose presence in us we become aware of more and more. It must not be thought, however, that building such a "meaningful interior world" is a purely subjective activity. On the contrary, it means a sharing in the *sensus fidelium* or what Paul calls "the mind of Christ": that is, the common interior life of all those who are led by the Spirit and who are faithful to God and to the gospel.

Meditatio not only analyzes the Word that is contained in the words of Scripture, it also at times must struggle with the Word. In his prayer at the Last Supper Jesus prayed to his Father:

> I gave them your Word
> and the world has hated them for it.

At times there is conflict between what God's Word tells us and what our culture has to say to us. It is a conflict that can cut through the very center of our hearts. We hear the call to discipleship and to a total following of Jesus; at the same time we hear other words calling us in different directions. These words can worm their way into our hearts and we have to face hard choices. What if our reflection on the Word of God threatens our security and the way of life we have become accustomed to? What if it calls for changes and risks we are not yet ready to make?

We may even feel betrayed by the Word and its demands and experience kinship with the reluctant prophet, Jeremiah. Indeed, there may be occasions when the gusty irreverence of his prayer fits us like a hair shirt. It's an emotional release to join him in saying: "You duped me, O Lord, and I let myself be duped." Yet there is no relief, for the Word of God can be irresistible. So, like the Prophet, we may experience that the Word is "like a fire" burning so strongly in our hearts that "we grow weary holding it in" (Jer. 20:7–9). Perhaps then, though only after long and arduous struggle, we at last surrender to the demands of the Word and experience — in a way that Jeremiah, it seems, did not — God's peace that comes from the Word that does not return to Him till it has accomplished the purposes for which He has sent it.

Some Scripture Texts

There is an expressive picture drawn in the Book of Revelation that reveals how the Word of God can be at once sweet and bitter. John, we are told, hears a voice from heaven telling him: "Go, take the open scroll from the hand of the angel standing on the sea and on the land." He went to the angel and asked for the scroll. The angel ordered him to take the scroll and eat it. John tells us:

> I took the scroll from the angel's hand
> and ate it.
> In my mouth it tasted sweet as honey,
> but when I swallowed it
> my stomach turned sour.
> Then someone said to me:
> "You must prophesy again
> for many peoples and nations, languages and kings."
> (10:10–11)

What the text is telling us is that the Word which can be a source of joy and peace in reflection can at times become sorrow, agony, pain, and struggle when we move from reflection to action. The scroll John ate, which was sweet on the lips and in his mouth, soured his stomach when he came to understand that it was calling him to preach a message that he knew would lead to suffering, persecution, perhaps even martyrdom. Yet, like Jeremiah centuries before him, he could not resist the drive of the Word: the Word that must accomplish its purposes.

This passage from Revelation speaks of the stomach as the place where the Word is digested; once digested the Word moves the Prophet to action. There is a Gospel parable (the parable of the Sower and the Seed) in Luke, chapter 8, which carries a similar message, though using different imagery. The sower scatters his seed (which we are told represents the Word of God) on different kinds of soil: rocky, briery, good. The good soil represents, Luke tells us, "those who hear the Word [*lectio*] in a spirit of openness [meditative reflection], retain it [meditative memory], and bear fruit through perseverance [action]" (8:15).

It is no great leap from this parable to the infancy narratives of Luke and his description of Jesus' most devoted disciple, his Mother. Following the visit of the Bethlehem shepherds and their revelation of what had happened to them, Luke tells us that "Mary treasured all these things and reflected on them in her heart" (2:19). Here also there is mention of reception into the heart and the memory ("treasured all these things") and reflective meditation ("reflected on them in her heart"). And all this was preliminary to what the Gospels do not narrate in any detail but clearly suppose: Mary's lifelong service to her Son. No wonder Jesus could say years later, in words that apply preeminently to Mary, "My mother and my brothers [and sisters] are those who hear the Word of God [*lectio* leading into *meditatio*] and act upon it" (8:21).

Background for Meditation:
Scriptural and Theological Themes

I have indicated that meditation means thinking about the words of Scripture, analyzing them, struggling with them, sometimes resisting them, sometimes being overcome by them. Our reaction to the words will depend in some measure on how these words "happen" to us as we read.

But the way the words "happen" to us will in turn depend, to a greater or lesser degree, on what we bring as background to the hearing of the Scriptures. Earlier I mentioned that study was not the same thing as meditation and could never be a substitute for it. At the same time study can be very helpful to us: first, it can help us know more clearly what the words of Scripture meant to those who wrote them and to those for whom they were first intended; and, secondly, it can make it easier for us to recognize what actually is happening when the Word "happens" to us in our *lectio* and *meditatio*.

I am not suggesting that we undertake at this point a course in Scripture. I would, however, like to venture something less ambitious, that is, a brief discussion of some major themes that thread their way through the Scriptures. Such a discussion will give us a context for reading the Scriptures. Discovering the context of Scripture means seeing the particular text or passage we are reading within the framework of other texts and passages that surround them or relate to them. This is an important undertaking, for we can understand the meaning of some portion of Scripture only when we see it in its proper context. A simple example will clarify what I mean.

Suppose you are sitting on the front porch of your home. A big black car drives up. A man gets out, walks toward you and says: "The house is green." Suppose, further, that you had never seen the man before. His words would be unintelligible to you. You would know the meaning of each of the four words in the sentence, but the sentence itself would be a big puzzle.

But imagine a different situation. Suppose you had decided

that your house had become too small for you and had made up your mind to buy a new one. You contact a real-estate agent. A few days later he calls you and says: "I have a house I think you will like. I'll pick you up and show it to you." A little later, you are sitting on the porch. A big black car drives up. A man gets out, walks toward you and says: "The house is green." You know exactly what he means. He is the real-estate agent and he is talking about the house he mentioned to you over the phone. You now know that the house he is going to show you is green.

Why is it that the same series of words that was unintelligible to you in the first situation becomes perfectly understandable in the second? The reason is simple: in the second situation that series of words had a context. They were part of the story of your life. They were in continuity with your previous action of calling the real-estate agent about searching for a house.

The Holy Scriptures tell a story: the story of God relating and revealing Himself to His people and becoming involved in their lives. They also tell the story of a people responding with varying, often alternating, degrees of fidelity and infidelity to their God. Particular texts or sections of Scripture take on meaning for us when we see how they fit into the whole narrative of that story. Certain words and ideas that run through the narrative are keys that help unlock the meaning of the story. They are special threads that serve to weave a pattern of meaning in the tapestry of that story.

Understanding these words and ideas will help us to understand better what the Scriptures were originally intended to say. Knowing this should enable us to see more clearly what God's Word is saying to us now. In a word, it should help us to meditate better.

There is yet one further aspect of the Scriptures that we need to consider. The words and ideas we find there reflect the understanding of God and Jesus and the divine will that emerge from the experience of the early Church. Yet you and I are some nineteen hundred years removed from that experience. It has not been thrown at us like a stone; it has been transmitted through history. The story that the Scripture tells did not stop when the last book of the canon was completed.

This being true, it is not enough that we see the words and ideas of the Scriptures in their own context; we have to see them also in the context of the lived experience of the Christian Church as in each age it has received and handed on the self-revelation of God and continued the Christian story. This lived experience of God's people is articulated (always imperfectly, for God's reality can never be adequately captured in human words) in what we call tradition. As each age hands on the tradition to the next, it leaves on it the impress of its own perceptions and insights. Some ages have enriched that tradition; others, it can probably be said, have impoverished it. Yet there is no other way in which it can come to us, and we have the confidence of faith that, in this process of handing down and handing over, the Holy Spirit is gradually leading us — even though at times we may seem to take one step backward as we take two forward — into all truth. This was Jesus' promise (see John 16:13).

I have chosen, then, to discuss in the next chapter some key words of Scripture and some basic theological themes with which our tradition has enriched these words. The approach will be moderately academic, though I hope not ponderously so. The intent will be practical: to help us in our meditating.

5

Some Biblical Words
and Theological Themes

This chapter, a kind of appendix to the previous one, is intended to offer some background that will facilitate our efforts to analyze and apply the Word of God as we meditate on it. Though longer than the chapter to which it is an appendix (!), it makes no pretense at any kind of completeness either in the words chosen for comments or the reflections (linguistic, scriptural, and theological) offered on these words. The choice of the words and the direction the reflections have taken undoubtedly betray my own interests and biases, which the reader who wishes to go on must, happily or unhappily, bear with.

1. The Gospel and the Gospels

The word "Gospel" means "good news" or "glad tidings." First of all it is "news," which means something that happens, an event that takes place in history. The *news* referred to in the Scriptures is God's intervention in history in a definitive way. His intervention is *good* news because it brings salvation and peace to people. The "Gospel" is never simply a supplying of historical information; it is a proclamation of salvation announced and achieved by God in Jesus Christ.

Jesus' Proclamation

Jesus understands his mission as the announcement of the "Good News" that God is about to intervene in history to establish His reign. Thus in the first of the *written* Gospels, Mark describes Jesus' inaugural sermon in this way: "Jesus appeared in Galilee proclaiming the Good News of God: 'This is the time of fulfillment. The reign of God is at hand. Reform your lives and believe in the Gospel.'" Mark tells us that Jesus proclaimed the "Good News" and that part of what he proclaimed was "believe in the Gospel." It should be noted that what is translated as "Good News" in one place and "Gospel" in the other is the same Greek word: *evangelion*.

In Matthew's gospel, when Jesus answers the messengers who come from John the Baptist with the question: "Are you 'He who is to come' or do we look for another?," he tells them to report to John what they have heard and seen: the blind recovering their sight, cripples walking, lepers being cured, deaf people hearing, the dead being raised and "*the poor having the good news preached to them*" (11:2–5).

The Church's Proclamation

If the "Good News," as Jesus proclaims it, is that God is in the process of entering in a definitive way into human history to establish His reign, the "Good News," as preached by the early Church, is that God has so intervened and He has done so in Jesus Christ. God acted to bring His salvation into the world especially when He raised Jesus from the dead. This is the heart of the "Good News" as it was preached by the Church. God's raising Jesus from the dead meant that Jesus entered into a new kind of human life. (See, below, "Eschatology" for further details.) More than that, it meant that Jesus, through the Spirit of God whom he could now send, was able to make it possible for all those who believe in him to enter into that same kind of immortal existence.

In the New Testament the word "Gospel" always refers to the *oral* proclamation of salvation and never to something fixed in writing. The New Testament knows only the one Gospel (the Gospel of salvation in Jesus Christ). To put "Gospel" into the plural would falsify its very nature. From the second century onward, however, there are references to *Gospels*, meaning the written accounts of the one Gospel.

The Written Gospels

These written "Gospels," of which there are a number, though only four have been accepted into the canon (i.e., the list of sacred books) by the Church, constitute a new literary genre. It would be a mistake to consider them as either historical or biographical writing—though obviously they are not without an element of history and biography. But the principal interest of the writers lies elsewhere. What is perhaps even more to the point, their sources lie outside the realm of strict history or biography. Their chief source was the oral preaching and teaching of the early Church. This oral "handing on"—the sole form for the transmission of the Gospel for a generation—included what Scripture scholars refer to as the *kerygma* and the *didache*.

The *kerygma* means, literally, the preaching directed to non-believers with the intention of bringing them to belief in Jesus Christ as the One through whom God saves. The heart of that preaching was the proclamation of the resurrection, preceded by a brief account of the ministry of Jesus beginning with his baptism by John the Baptist. Samples of this early preaching can be found in the sermons of Peter that are given in the early chapters of the Acts of Apostles (see, for instance, Acts, chapter 10). The preaching of the resurrection was accompanied by an invitation to baptism, which was the means of entrance into the Christian community (the *koinonia*). Once people had accepted baptism and entered the community, they needed to be instructed in more detail on what it meant to live the new life in

Christ. This instruction, directed to believers, was called the *didache*. The early Church, in presenting the *didache*, drew on the memories of those who had been eyewitnesses of the sayings and deeds of Jesus.

Very early — perhaps a few decades after the death-resurrection event — a number of the sayings of Jesus were apparently put into writing — probably for catechetical purposes — but without regard for the context in which these sayings were spoken. Then, some time just before or after the destruction of Jerusalem (A.D. 70), a written work appeared that we call the Gospel of Mark. Its outline is the *kerygma*: from the baptism of Jesus to the passion-resurrection events. Into that basic framework, the author incorporates some of the deeds and sayings of Jesus as they had been handed down in the *didache*.

Some twenty years or so after Mark's Gospel, two other Gospels appeared: Matthew and Luke. They appear to draw on the collection of sayings already referred to, which they fit into the basic pattern of what a Gospel is that had already been established in Mark. Still later a quite different, though complementary, presentation of the *kerygma* and the *didache* appears that we know as the Gospel of John. Because the first three Gospels follow the same basic outline, they are sometimes called the "Synoptic Gospels," synoptic meaning "seeing something from the same or similar point of view."

The Uniqueness of Each Gospel
Though there was a time when it was fashionable to think of the Gospel writers as mere redactors who collected materials from the early Church's preaching and teaching, Scripture scholars are generally agreed today that this represents an oversimplified view. Far from being mere compilers, those who put the four Gospels together present their material with their own unique insight and vision. These different and mutually enriching views of Jesus and his mission help to deepen our un-

derstanding of the meaning of God's saving actions done for us in Jesus. It is becoming clearer too that, not only is it true that John differs from the Synoptics, but that the three Synoptics differ from one another considerably more than was once thought. That is why some contemporary scholars are beginning to frown on the use of the word "synoptic" as failing to do justice to the rich uniqueness of each of these Gospels.

The Gospels as Faith-Documents

Because the written Gospels are neither historical nor biographical in any strict sense of those terms, but rather enshrine the early preaching and teaching of the Church as it was handed down orally, we must conclude that it is seldom, if ever, that we have in the Gospels the exact words of Jesus. More than that, we need also to keep in mind that the Gospels are "confessing documents," in other words, documents written by people who believed that Jesus was the Risen One, that he was Messiah and Lord. This faith in Jesus — which was a postresurrection experience — is sometimes projected back into their telling of the narrative of Jesus' sayings and actions. For instance, when the Gospel writers tell the story of the feeding miracle, they are already members of a Christian community who celebrate the Eucharist in memory of the Lord Jesus and with the consciousness of his presence among them as they celebrate. Hence when they tell the story of the feeding miracle, they describe Jesus as using Eucharistic gestures: he "takes" the bread, "looks up" to heaven, "breaks" the bread, "distributes" it to the people.

The Gospels, in other words, are by no means "neutral" documents. When the Gospel writers describe the ministry of Jesus, their descriptions are colored by their Easter faith. When they describe the deeds of the Carpenter of Nazareth and narrate his words, they know what the people of the time of Jesus' ministry did not know: namely, that he is Messiah and God's

Son. The starting point, therefore, for the Gospel writers is the resurrection of Jesus. The Gospels quite literally were written backward. By this I mean that the passion-resurrection narratives were the first part of the Gospel story to be put into writing. Then an account of Jesus' ministry, written in the light of Easter faith, was prefixed to these narratives. Finally — and a good bit later — the infancy narratives were written. It is significant that the earliest of the Gospels, Mark's, has no infancy narrative and has sometimes been referred to as a passion narrative with a preface. Matthew and Luke both have infancy narratives but with significant differences one from another. The fourth Gospel goes back much farther even than the infancy: to the Word of God in the bosom of the Father.

Levels of Meaning

In reading the Gospels, the reader is able to look for three levels of meaning: (1) the historical level: the meaning of what Jesus said and did during the time of his ministry; (2) the community level: the meaning given to the words and deeds of Jesus as they were used by the early Church in its preaching and teaching in that period between the end of Jesus' earthly life and the time when the Gospels came to be written; and (3) the level of the written word: the meaning that the Gospel-writers give to this material in the light of their own understanding of Jesus and his mission. It should be immediately clear that the only level that is immediately attainable in reading the Gospels is the third level. The other two have to be "reconstructed" from the third.

Perhaps there may be some who might feel somehow "cheated" if they are no longer able to recover the exact words and deeds of Jesus. Yet if we reflect for a moment on the fact that, in lieu of historically accurate reportings of events, we have the Spirit-filled remembrances of the early Christian community, we may come to see that to possess the Gospels is much more enriching than it would have been to have "stenographic reports" about Jesus. Father Barnabas Ahern has expressed this beautifully in his book *New Horizons* (Notre Dame: Fides, 1963). He writes:

> An example may help to make all this clear. The floor of the ocean is littered with sea shells. Only some of these are swept onto the shore. There wind and rain smooth away rough edges. The sunlight brings out rich coloring. A person finds them there, gathers them up and forms them into a vase, beautiful in shape and color. To appreciate the exquisite beauty of the vase we not only gaze at its whole contour and color-pattern but we study also the graceful turn and delicate tint of every shell.
>
> It is the same with the Gospels. Our Lord's life was like an ocean bed filled with words and deeds in such abundance that books could not contain them. Only some of these reached the shore of the primitive community. There the wind and light of the Spirit shaped the telling of each deed and illumined its deeper meaning. The Evangelists gathered together these living memories and molded them into a Gospel under the light of the Spirit. No two Gospels are the same: each has its own contour and coloring.
>
> To measure the truth and to appreciate the beauty of the Gospel we cannot be content to study merely the formative work of the Evangelist and the over-all impression of his literary composition. We must also study each unit in the Gospel, as we would study each shell in the vase, to discover what the Holy Spirit disclosed to the Church—the full meaning of each event and the vital significance of each word in the life of Jesus. (pp. 83-84)

The Holy Spirit, we believe, is present in the Church to enable us to understand the Word of God, but that presence is not confined to the primitive era of the Church or to any past age. When we read Scripture, therefore, our task is not simply to search out what Scripture may have meant in ages past; we need to know what it says to members of the contemporary Christian community.

In the second and third chapters of the Book of Revelation, we hear the words of the "One Who was dead but now lives forever and ever": words addressed in letter-form to the seven churches of Asia Minor as they existed near the turn of the first century. Each letter concludes with the admonition: "Let the one who has ears heed the Spirit's word to the churches." As the Spirit spoke *then* to different churches in an area that comprised part of the Church universal, and called all the churches to listen to what the Spirit was saying to each of them, so we are called *now* to heed what the Spirit says among the churches in our day. The Spirit's word is not a word of the past; it is always the contemporary word.

At the end of a reading in the Liturgy of the Word, we usually say: "This is the Word of the Lord." Sometimes I feel the inclination to add "at least I hope so." Having the words of Scripture read in our presence is not the same thing as truly heeding the Word. We have to let the Word "happen" to us in all its power. We have to reflect on it, let it take possession of us, be imprinted on our memories and move us to action. Only then can it be genuinely true that: "This is the Word of the Lord," or "This is the Gospel of the Lord."

2. The Kingdom (Reign) of God (Gk. *Basileia*)

The "kingdom of God" is the central theme of Jesus' preaching in the Synoptics. More recent translations tend to render the Greek word *basileia* as "reign" rather than kingdom, since the word refers more to sovereignty than territory. The word's meaning does vary, however, and in some cases the notion of "reign" spills over into "realm." In these cases *basileia* may justifiably be translated as "kingdom."

For the Synoptic Gospels the ministry of Jesus is the definitive in-breaking into the world of the "reign" of God with its
power to heal, to save, and to restore. The *miracles* of Jesus are
signs of the power of the kingdom working through him. In
fact, in describing Jesus' marvelous deeds, the Synoptics use
the Greek word *dynamis*, which means "power." God's power is
unmistakably at work in Jesus. The *parables* of Jesus are not
intended to inculcate moral lessons, but to expound the challenge posed by the kingdom. The parables speak about the
character of the kingdom, its growth and the demands it makes
on those who wish to enter. Yet entrance into the kingdom is a
matter of personal choice. Unlike the reign of Caesar, the reign
of God is established by the free surrender that men and wom-
en make to His sovereignty.

The ambiguity in the description of the kingdom as something
that is already "near" or already "arrived" and "in our midst" and
at the same time as something that is "yet to come" is to some
degree resolved if we see the kingdom as a reality that has indeed
come among us and yet is operative in the world and moving
inevitably toward a fulfillment of cosmic scope.

The kingdom reaches a point of climactic manifestation, and
at the same time of profound hiddenness in the total obedience
of Jesus, an obedience even unto death on a cross. Because of
his obedience, God exalts him by raising him to a new and
immortal existence. As the Risen One, Jesus is the presence in
the world of the eschatologically victorious grace of God. By
this I mean that the grace of God, which will be fully victorious
at the end of time, is already present in Jesus and in him is
operative in the world and moving toward the consummation of
which Paul speaks:

> When finally, all has been subjected to the Son, he will then
> subject himself to the One who made all things subject to him,
> so that God may be all in all. (1 Cor. 15:28)

The Kingdom and the Church (Gk. *Ekklesia*)

The Church is related to the kingdom, but the two must not be identified. The grace of the kingdom is operative in the whole world, not just in the Church. The Church is the communion (*koinonia*) of those who are called together by God (*ekklesia*) and who profess that "Jesus is Lord." The Church is that place where the world can become aware of its true destiny. The grace of God is experienced in the Church and the Church is the instrument of the kingdom.

But it is not the only instrument of the kingdom nor is it the only place where grace is experienced. The grace of God is active in the whole world. The Pastoral Constitution on the Church in the Modern World (*Gaudium et Spes*) of Vatican II tells us in number 22 that grace works in an unseen way in the hearts of all people of good will. It explains:

> For, since Christ died for all men and women and since the ultimate vocation of human persons is one, and divine, we ought to believe that the Holy Spirit in a manner known only to God offers to every person the possibility of being associated with the paschal mystery.

God is master of His gifts. He saves through the Church, but He can save without the Church. This does not make the Church unimportant, but it relativizes it in its relation to the absoluteness of God and His kingdom.

The Church is the sign of that grace of God operating in the whole world. That is why a theology of the Church has to begin with a consideration of the Church as the sign or sacrament of Christ and the kingdom he inaugurated, rather than the Church as an institution. Our primary duty in the Church is not loyalty to the institution, but fidelity to Christ and to the kingdom of God that he embodies. I intend that not as an anti-institutional statement, but a perspective-giving one, establishing priorities. If the Church exists to be the sign of Christ acting in the world to bring the kingdom to fulfillment, then she cannot center attention on herself or her structure. This would belie her character as a sign. A sign points to another. The Church must point not to herself but to Christ and to the kingdom he inaugurated.

The French scholar and priest Loisy, who was excommunicated from the Church for "Modernism" in the early years of the present century, once said: "Jesus promised us the kingdom and we got the Church instead." There is some truth in this rather acid criticism. One of the tendencies the Church has had to resist all through her history — and history witnesses that she has not always been successful — has been the tendency to identify the Church with the kingdom. This kind of triumphalism betrays both the church and the kingdom. For the kingdom, in its final realization, denotes fullness and consummation. This is never achieved in the Church. The life of the Church always involves the tension between the "already" and the "not yet." Her mission is to continue building the kingdom, yet praying at her Lord's command: "Thy kingdom come." For the kingdom of God is essentially an eschatological reality: an event that God will bring about in the end times. It will come only when the universal lordship of Jesus is acknowledged, when he is able to hand over the kingdom to the Father, and God will be all in all.

Every time we celebrate the Eucharist, we distinguish kingdom and Church when we say the beautiful prayer in which we ask Jesus for his peace. We entreat him: "Look not on our sins, but on the faith of your *Church*, and grant us the peace and unity of your *kingdom* where you live forever and ever."

3. Eschatology

Derived from the Greek word *eschaton*, which means "the end days" — all those things that will happen at the end when history has run its course — eschatology is the biblical understanding that history is not a cyclic turning around itself, but a linear movement toward a goal that is God's ultimate purpose for creation. In the prophetic literature of the Hebrew Scriptures, the final accomplishment of God's purposes will take place decisively on "the Day of the Lord."

The distinctive contribution of New Testament eschatology is the conviction that in the history of Jesus Christ, especially in his being raised from the dead, God's decisive eschatological act has already taken place. Yet it has happened in such a way that a final consummation remains still in the future. Hence in the New Testament there is a *realized* eschatology: "the Day of the Lord" has arrived in Jesus; there is also a *futurist* eschatology: the final fulfillment of God's saving action when the kingdom of God will be fully realized is still to come.

Eschatology and the Resurrection of Jesus

It is important to understand that the New Testament writers see the resurrection of Jesus as an eschatological event. His risen life does not mean a return to mortality but entrance into the immortal life that belongs to the end days. There is a sense in which it could be said that when God raised Jesus from the dead, eschatology became history. Because it was an eschatological event, the resurrection released Jesus from the restrictions of time and space, which are the accompaniments of historical existence; yet because it happened not at the end of history but in the middle of it, the resurrection impinged on our world of time and space and continues to do so. The Risen One is no longer confined to our world and the limitations that mortal existence imposes. Transcending the world, he yet belongs to it, to all history and to all peoples. He is the contemporary of every age.

With the raising of Jesus, resurrection ceased to be merely an object of hope that men and women looked forward to in a future that was beyond history. Not only did Jesus enter into a new existence but he also calls his own to share in that existence: not in a distant future, but *now*. Through him we have already received the life that will never end. Our participation in the paschal mystery, begun in baptism, lived in our daily lives and celebrated in the Eucharist, means that the grave can never hold us captive: our death will mean that we shall enter fully into the kind of life he already lives in God.

Parousia

The final eschatological hope centers in the *parousia*, or the "Second Coming of Christ." This is the New Testament equivalent of the Prophets' "Day of the Lord." In fact, in a number of places it becomes "the Day of the Lord Jesus." It seems clear that the early Christians believed in an imminent *parousia* and lived in daily expectation of the Lord's return. Some of the parables that deal with "being ready" and "awake" for the master's return express this sense of imminence. When it came to be realized that the *parousia* would be delayed, these parables about readiness had to be reinterpreted to apply to the grace-filled coming of the Lord in the ministry of the Church.

It is worth pointing out that, while theologically *parousia* points to the future (a coming), etymologically it refers more to the present. It derives from two Greek words: the preposition *para*, which means "alongside of," and the noun *ousia*, "being," a derivative of the verb *eimi*, which means "to be." In classical Greek *parousia* is used to describe the *coming* of a ruler to an area of his kingdom to *be present* among his people. His *parousia* means that he is "alongside of" his people, that is, "with them." But to be with them he has to come to them. "Being with" is a result of coming. In the Latin Vulgate the Greek word *parousia* is translated by *adventus*. Hence *Advent*, which we generally translate as "coming," is the same word as *parousia*. One "comes" in order to "be present."

Parousia and the Contemplative

The deepest meaning of *parousia* is not that God will one day come in Jesus, but that, in the risen Jesus, He is already present among us. The God who is transcendent becomes known in Jesus as the God who is immanent. The God who is Wholly Other is experienced in Jesus as the God who is at our side.

The problem of the *parousia* is not primarily one of time on the part of Jesus, that is, when and how he is going to come; rather it is a problem of awakened consciousness on our part. God in Jesus is already totally at our side, but we are not yet totally and completely aware of His presence. When we — all of us — achieve this total awareness of His presence, so that nothing separates us from Him, it will be as if Jesus has come a second time.

The "Second Coming," therefore, speaks not so much of something that is going to happen to Jesus, but of something that is in the process of happening to us. There is a sense in which we can say that the "Second Coming" is a metaphor or a symbol. For Jesus as the Risen One is forever a part of the human condition, which means that he cannot really come into the world a second time. He is already fully and totally present in it.

This understanding has deep implications for the contemplative. For the goal of contemplation is to enable us to experience the presence of God. It is an awakening, a becoming aware of what is really there. When we become fully awake and aware, it will be as if the Second Coming has happened. We shall know that nothing has happened and yet everything has happened.

4. *Metanoia*: Conversion, Repentance

In Jesus' inaugural proclamation, as Mark presents it, the announcement that the "kingdom" is at hand is followed by the call: "Repent [i.e., be converted] and believe in the Gospel." We have discussed "Gospel" and "kingdom" above. It is in the context of these understandings that I wish to speak of *metanoia* or "conversion."

The etymology of the word *metanoia* is helpful toward understanding this meaning-packed word. It derives from *nous*, a Greek noun that means "mind," "insight," "intuition," and *meta*, a Greek preposition that means "after" or "around." *Metanoia* can be understood, in literal fashion, to mean "after-knowledge" that leads to a "turning around" of one's insights or views. If this new understanding of things carries with it the feeling that one's previous view was foolish, improper, or evil, *metanoia* may include a sense of remorse, regret, and sorrow for previous thoughts, plans, and actions. Such remorse would normally bring with it the realization that faults must be corrected, together with the resolve to effect such correction.

In classical Greek, *metanoia* was act-*metanoia*, by which I mean that it applied to a change in certain modes of action, but was never understood as a radical change in the whole of one's conduct.

New Testament Meaning of Conversion

It is this latter notion that dominates the biblical understanding of *metanoia*. This is true of the Prophets (with their call to Israel to "return to the Lord your God") and of John the Baptist who calls his hearers to break with an ungodly and sinful past and undergo a genuine inner change. *Metanoia* was also basic to Jesus' preaching of the kingdom. His call to repentance differs from John's in that John's call to repentance is in view of "one who is to come" (a wrathful one!), whereas the call of Jesus to conversion follows from his announcement that the eschatological *basileia* (see above) is already present in his own person; he is the "one who has come" and he comes, not in wrath, but to save. That is why his call to conversion is followed not by a threat (as in the preaching of John), but by the joyful invitation to believe in the "Good News."

Metanoia flows, therefore, from God's definitive revelation of

Himself in Jesus, which demands a final and unconditional decision of the part of men and women. This decision must affect the whole person: the very inner core and center of his/her life as well as his/her total behavior in thoughts, words, and acts. *Metanoia* is not a human achievement but a gift of God—a gift that never ceases to make demands on us. We are able to receive the gift only if we become like children—little, receptive, ready to let God work in us.

Conversion is not a once-and-for-all experience, but a continuous imperative of the Christian life. Nor is it necessarily experienced in a single event or in one whose effect is instantaneous. It may be a long-term experience or a series of experiences whose cumulative effect brings about a genuine turning toward a more authentic commitment to the Lord Jesus and his Gospel. The Hebrew equivalent of *metanoia* is *shuvh*, which means a 180-degree turn toward God. This may be a helpful way of looking at the conversion experience: turning so completely from self that we are face to face with God. To move from having self as the center of my life to having God as that center is indeed a 180-degree turn. And it takes time—and grace.

Some Conversion Experiences

To illustrate what I mean I would like to recall what I consider three key conversion experiences in my life. One such conversion took place in the late 1950s and the early 1960s when, through contact with contemporary biblical scholarship (a contact that came through reading and attendance at numerous biblical institutes at which I met some of the truly distinguished biblical scholars of our times) and spurred on by the responsibility I had of teaching courses in Scripture at Nazareth College, I discovered the Bible in a completely new and thrilling way. Until that time the only approach to the Bible I had known was that which had been typical of Roman Catholic seminaries in the 1940s and in many decades previous: the way of *text-proofing*. Text-proofing means that isolated biblical passages are torn from their context and used to substantiate conclusions already arrived at from extra-biblical sources. This way of viewing the Bible assumes that it is a series of detached aphorisms that have a kind of eternal meaning without relationship to the historical and human context in which they were written.

The biblical movement that came into its own in Roman Catholic circles in the 1950s and 1960s helped me to understand that the Bible was indeed God's self-revelation, but carried in the fragile vessels of time-conditioned documents written by authors who were products of their history and who shared the mentality of their times. This meant that literary and historical criticism, with all that this involved, was necessary before we could really grasp the message the Bible has for us. Then, once we knew what the Scriptures were saying to their own times, we would be better prepared to relate its meaning to our own age and circumstances. For the first time I was really *reading* the Bible to hear what it said, instead of *using* it to prove what I already knew. This was a truly liberating experience: it opened up the whole world of the Bible for me — truly for the first time. It was an experience of conversion to a new way of listening to God.

A second conversion in my life, prepared for by the first, came out of the Second Vatican Council, as I followed its deliberations, read the documents it produced, and saw the beginnings of the renewal and transformation of the Church that it envisioned. What this "conversion" involved for me was a movement from a theological rigidity that thought all theological issues had already been settled to an open-ended vision of theology that saw it as a task continually in process, never fully completed and in constant need of rethinking and rearticulation.

My "third conversion," which would probably have been impossible without the first two, was a "conversion" to nonviolence. For most of my life I had taken for granted that the

"Catholic position" on war was the principle of the "just war." Though I knew that it had originated in non-Christian sources (with people like the Stoic philosophers and the Latin writer Cicero), it was sufficient for me — for a long time at least — that it had been "baptized" by Christian theologians (like Augustine and Aquinas) and was in possession in the Catholic Church. But my reading of the New Testament (especially Jesus' words about love for all, including enemies), the influence of the Second Vatican Council with its limited but genuine endorsement of nonviolence, my intensive study of the writings of Thomas Merton, and my contact with some of his correspondents (notably Hildegard Goss-Mayr) who were committed to nonviolence — all these factors have moved me to an entirely new way of understanding not only war, but the way I must live my whole life. Nonviolence is no longer an option for me that I may choose or not. It has become for me an essential part of my following of Christ. I may not always measure up to its demands, but I know it is the ideal that I cannot cease to strive for in every area of my life.

Metanoia and *Pistis* (Faith)

Metanoia establishes us in a new personal relationship with God — a relationship of faith. In the preaching of Jesus (in the Synoptics) faith is not a second requirement for entrance into the kingdom; rather it is the outgrowth of conversion. It is, as it were, the positive side of *metanoia*.

If for Jesus conversion includes faith, it may be said that in the Pauline letters *metanoia* is absorbed into Paul's central concept of salvation by faith. For Paul conversion means what faith means: "being in Christ," "dying and rising with him," being "a new creation." In the Johannine writings the notion of conversion tends to be expressed in very positive terms: "new life in Christ," "passing from death to life, from darkness to light," "victory of truth over falsehood, love over hate."

In the New Testament conversion does not mean submission to a law, but surrender to God. The Law of the kingdom is the Law of the Spirit that can never be adequately articulated in any written code of laws. (See further discussion of law.)

Conversion and Contemplation

Understanding the meaning of conversion is helpful in coming to know what contemplation is. If conversion means a total change, it must include a transformation of consciousness as well as of behavior. The goal of contemplation is nothing less than a transformation of consciousness, that is, it transforms the way we experience God and all else that is. Through contemplation one experiences the deepest meaning of *metanoia*.

5. Law

Law in Israel

The various law codes that come down from Israel's earliest history find parallels in their contents with similar codes that existed among neighboring peoples. No parallel has been discovered, however, to the context in which Israel put its laws. That context was the covenant given them by their God who in His gracious goodness had chosen them to be His people. Israel's Laws, therefore, were covenant stipulations specifying, in very concrete detail, how Israel was to express its gratitude toward God for His mighty deeds on their behalf, especially His greatest deed—which epitomized the rest—His deliverance of them from the slavery of Egypt into freedom.

Israel before the Exile

Fundamental, then, to Israel's understanding of its own self-identity was the realization that it was a society governed by God's will (expressed in the stipulations of the covenant codes) and that its history would be determined by its fidelity or infidelity to the covenant stipulations.

In the sixth century B.C., a repentant people—in exile in Babylon—confessed that it had taken the road of disobedience and infidelity and that the exile was the punishment of a just and righteous God for their infidelities.

While they lived in exile, they were without temple or sacrifice. All that was left to them of their ancient heritage was the very Law that they had transgressed. The Law (the Torah) became the mainstay of Jewish life. Happiness was to be found not simply in its observance but also in its study. Some of the exilic Psalms express this delight in the law: Psalm 119, for instance, runs on for 176 verses, each in different ways praising the greatness of the Law. Removed from its covenant context, the law came to be viewed as eternally existing and immutable. The rabbis spoke of it among the beings that existed before creation. In fact, so holy was the Torah that—as I mentioned earlier—some rabbis taught that God Himself took time out to study it. The Pharisees understood the obligations imposed by the law in the strictest sense. To make sure that the law was perfectly observed, they "built fences" around the law, that is, they advanced the obligation of the law beyond the sense of the words to make it more difficult to violate it.

Postexilic Israel

After the return from exile the law remained the dominant reality in the life of the Jewish people. The Law was expanded: interpretations of the Law, which included the "fences around the law," formed an "oral Law" that was put on a par with the written law and, eventually, attributed to Moses. Even the restored temple could not compete with the Law. In fact, the services carried out in the temple were done precisely because they were prescribed in the Law. There was even a radical rethinking of the covenant: it came to be seen as the reward

God gave to His people for good behavior. If preexilic Israel saw the covenant as a gift of God's graciousness to an Israel that was without merit, postexilic Israel witnessed a growing belief that the covenant had been given as a reward for fidelity to the Law. Ben Sirach (44:20) says of Abraham: "He observed the precepts of the Most High and entered into covenant with him." John Bright, commenting on the tendency thus to absolutize the law, refers to these words of Ben Sirach:

> Here law has ceased to be the definition of the requisite response to the gracious acts of God and become the means by which men might achieve the divine favor and become worthy of the promises. (*A History of Israel* [Philadelphia: Westminster, 1959], p. 428)

The doctrine of salvation as an unmerited gift of a gracious God has been changed into a doctrine of salvation through the works of the law. The conflict between these two ways of understanding law was to become one of the principal issues of struggle in the early Christian Church and has remained at issue throughout much of Christian history.

Jesus and the Law

Jesus' attitude toward the law was one of acceptance, but with some important reservations. He himself observed the law and denied the charge that he violated it. When he was so accused (e.g., for breaking the Sabbath by curing people on this day of rest), he always insisted that it was the oral Law and not the written Torah on which the charge was based.

There were a number of reservations in Jesus' attitude toward the Law.

1. He refused to be bound by the letter of the law, if obedience to a literal understanding of the law clearly violated its spirit. This is one way of interpreting his words in Matthew

5:17: "Do not think that I have come to abolish the law and the prophets. I have come, not to abolish them, but to fulfill them." It should be noted that Jesus does not say that he came to keep the law, but to *fulfill* it. To *keep* the law may mean simply doing what the law says. To *fulfill* the law means to achieve what the law intends. Jesus was continually telling the religious leaders of his day that they were keeping the Sabbath law but not fulfilling it.

It is possible today for a Roman Catholic to *keep* the Sunday law by "going to Mass" sometime between Saturday's sunset and Sunday's. One can do this, however, without *fulfilling* the intent of the Sunday observance — which is to make this day one of special praise to God for His gracious goodness and a day for remembering the wondrous mystery of the resurrection.

Jesus reinterprets the law. He moves us to look beyond what the law *says* in order to discover what it *means*. In thus transcending the law and the overly literalist approach to it, Jesus was in reality returning to a very important tradition in Israel, but one that was all but lost after the return from the exile: the tradition of the Law of the heart expressed so eloquently by Jeremiah and Ezechiel. These two Prophets — some six centuries before Jesus — spoke of the New Covenant that God would give His people: a Covenant in which the law would be written not on tablets of stone but on the human heart. God had said to Jeremiah (31:33): "I will give them a new spirit. I will place my law within them and write it upon their hearts."

Jesus firmly rejected legalism; such a mentality, which sees only what the law *prescribes* and not what it is *meant to achieve*, misses the fundamental point that law is not just a call to do something: in its deepest aspect it is a call to become something: to grow in love and commitment. The law, if you will, is not a *ceiling* beyond which we need not go; rather it is a *floor* on which we stand. It is a support from which we can reach out to do more and more for God and for our sisters and brothers.

2. Jesus insists on setting priorities among laws. Not all are

of equal importance. One of the dangers in legalism is forgetting this. Jesus insisted on the priority of the law of love. Love of God and neighbor sums up all the laws. It is by the love they have for one another that Jesus' disciples will be clearly identified. Love incorporates the disciple into the very life of God who is love.

3. Jesus refused to allow that obedience to the law was salvific. Though this teaching is more strongly emphasized in the Pauline letters, it is also very clear in the Gospels. The parable about the Pharisee and the taxcollector (Luke 17:9–14) is an obvious example. The Pharisee boasts of his exact observance of the law. The taxcollector begs for the forgiveness of God, even as he recognizes in his sinfulness that he has no claim to it whatsoever. Jesus says of the taxcollector: "This man went home from the temple justified, but the other did not."

Jesus claimed that the salvific power that the rabbis attributed to the law was given to him by the Father. It is he who saves, not the Law. That is why in his preaching he proclaims not new laws, but Gospel. He calls his disciples to reach for the highest perfection, in fact to become perfect as the Father is perfect. He proclaims high ideals to strive for and sets goals to be reached, but he does not legislate.

A good case could be made for saying that the only law he "promulgated" was not really a law but the invitation and challenge that he called "his commandment":

> This is my commandment:
> Love one another
> As I have loved you.

The Sermon on the Mount might, at a superficial reading, seem to contain precepts that are new laws. Yet they are much better understood, in the whole context of Jesus' sayings, as "Gospel" rather than "Law." By that I mean that the Sermon on the Mount is a stirring description, in concrete detail, of what one should be able to see in a disciple of Jesus. But the "precepts" of the Sermon, while they are by no means broad generalities, are not laws that can be viewed as direct regulations for behavior. Yet at the same time it must be said that it would be wrong to think that Jesus did not intend us to take them seriously. C. H. Dodd, in his brief but excellent book *Gospel and Law* (Cambridge University Press, 1950) offers us a helpful and healthy perspective. He writes about Jesus' command of love: "It is an obligation to reproduce in human action the *quality* and the *direction* of the act of God by which we are saved" (p. 71). He goes on to say about the precepts of Jesus contained in the Sermon on the Mount:

> I suggest that we may regard each of these precepts as indicating in a dramatic picture of some actual situation, the *quality* and *direction* which shall conform to the standard set by the divine *agape*. The quality may be present in its degree at a quite low level of achievement. The right direction may be clearly discernible in the act, even though the goal may be still far off. But the demand that our action in concrete situations should have *this* direction and *this* quality is categorical. (pp. 73–74)

Dodd suggests that one might compare, say, the command to give tithes (as the law of Moses required) and the precept of the Sermon on the Mount "to love one's enemies." You can know quite readily whether or not you have fulfilled the tithing command. If you give less than 10 percent you have disobeyed the law. If you give precisely 10 percent you have obeyed the law. If you wish to give 12 percent, that is your affair. The "precepts" of the Sermon on the Mount are quite different in character. Thus, for instance, there is no way in which you can say about the precepts of the Sermon (e.g., love of enemies) what the young man in the Gospel said about the Ten Commandments: "All these I have kept from my childhood" (Mark 10:20).

This way of reading the sayings of Jesus in the Gospel is of paramount importance. It can help one to see why many scripture scholars and theologians today are questioning whether or not Jesus taught the indissolubility of marriage as an absolute law or as a goal and an ideal that all married couples are called to strive for with all their strength. People may marry who intend to work toward that goal. Yet the situation may arise, wherever the fault may lie or perhaps without anyone being able to identify whose the fault may be, that a marriage relationship may die and existentially no longer exist. Some are asking today: should this be seen as the breaking of a law that rules out any further marriage so much so that such a marriage would put a person outside the pale of the Church? Or is it possible to see this first marriage as the failure to reach an ideal to which Jesus calls: a failure that must be admitted, that is deeply regrettable, that calls for repentance. Yet can it be said that this failure does not necessarily exclude the possibility of entering into another marriage that perhaps may be more mature and offer greater possibility of working toward the ideal that Jesus set? This is a highly debated question today, and I do not really wish to get into it at any length in a book on prayer (though neither do I want to avoid it completely, for prayer is about life and the problems it often brings). My intent here is simply to use it as an example of what Dodd means (and I agree with him) that the percepts of the Sermon on the Mount, as well as other precepts of Jesus, suggest the quality and direction our actions must have. But they are not in any sense laws in the way that the code laws of the Old Covenant are laws.

Paul and the Law

For Paul, as for Jesus, the Gospel takes primacy over any law. He is expressing his fundamental perspective when he writes to the Romans: "You are no longer under law, but under the grace of God" (6:14). A convert from Pharisaeism, Paul attributed to the grace of God manifested in Jesus Christ the salvific role that the Pharisees attributed to observance of the law.

His theological stance was worked out in the heat of controversy with the Judaizers, Christians of Jewish background, who insisted the Gentile Christians were bound equally with themselves to observe the law of Moses. Paul develops his position polemically in the Epistle to the Galatians and in a more theoretical and analytic fashion in Romans. Central to his theology is that we are saved not by doing the works of the law, but by faith in Jesus Christ. Faith must become active in love and the law may indicate some of the ways in which we can love. But nothing we do can be the cause of our salvation. We can only accept it as a gift from God.

One of the chief tasks of Paul's ministry was energetically to oppose those Christians who would attempt to substitute the way of a written code for the way of the Spirit, the external law for the inner life-giving law of the Spirit. Thus he writes, again to the Romans:

> We are discharged from the law
> to serve God in a new way:
> the way of the Spirit,
> in contrast to the old way:
> the way of a written code. (7:6)

To seek salvation through the observance of an external written code, no matter how holy that code might be, was for Paul a denial of the Gospel and a reversion to the Old Testament.

In every age the temptation is very strong to want to have a code of laws, precisely detailed, whose observance can give one the assurance of salvation. The New Testament call to accept salvation as a gift of God's love and then to live a life of love, in which the details of love's demands are never fully spelled out for us, is an invitation to freedom and personal responsibility that not every one relishes. Yet it is an invitation that is written broad across the pages of the New Testament.

6. *Christology*

A centerpiece in all three of the Synoptic Gospels is the twofold question put by Jesus to his disciples: (1) who do others say that I am? and (2) who do you say that I am? These are questions that Christians in every age have had to answer. They are questions we have to answer in our day.

The first question is the *theological* one. To answer it, we need to look at the creeds and doctrines that tell us what the Church has taught authoritatively about Jesus through the centuries. We need also to look at what theologians and saints and mystics have had to say about him. This accumulated wisdom of the Christian community, past and present, can enrich our insights into the meaning of what we shall never fully understand: the mystery of Jesus.

The second question: who do *you* say that I am? is the *existential* one. Because it is a deeply personal question, it cannot be answered simply in terms of theological categories. We can only answer it when, fortified surely by the wisdom of the whole Christian community, we yet speak out of our own experience as we have met the Lord Jesus in our daily efforts to live the Gospel.

The theological question about Jesus' identity centers about the mystery of One who is at once human and divine. We can say these words, but what do they mean? This is the theological task.

Moments of Christological Awareness

It will be helpful in understanding the nature of the theological task to look at the early Church in order to see how the earliest disciples of Jesus came gradually to understand who he was. One way to approach this is to note how the Gospels seem to suggest that there were various significant moments of "Christological awareness" in the experience of the early Christians.

By a "moment of Christological awareness" I mean a point in the life of the Church when the identity of Jesus as Messiah and Son of God came to be known or came to be understood more deeply. The Gospels seem to suggest that there was a gradual "pushing back" of the moment of Christological awareness.

In the earliest days of the Church's life, the initial "moment of Christological awareness" seems to have been the moment when they came to believe in the resurrection, that is to say, when they came to accept that, through the power of the Father, Jesus was raised from the dead and thus made to be "Messiah and Lord." This is the language you find in the earliest preaching of the Church (for instance in the kerygmatic sermons in Acts): Jesus "made to be Messiah and Lord." The language is clumsy, even inaccurate, by later ways of speaking. But it makes clear that it was in the experience of the Risen One that the disciples of Jesus first came to know his true identity.

As the Church reflected on the mystery of Jesus, the moment of Christological awareness was pushed back into the period of the ministry of Jesus. The Christological moment became the baptism of Jesus. It was at this moment, the Church came to realize, that Jesus received the full outpouring of God's Spirit and truly came to be realized as "the beloved Son of the Father."

The Gospels of Matthew and Luke, with the infancy narratives that they alone recount, push the Christological moment back to the time of Jesus's conception: he who is virginally conceived is already the Son of God. The Fourth Gospel takes the final step: pushing the Christological moment back into eternity: Jesus is the preexistent Son of the Father.

Moments of growth in Christological awareness were not confined to New Testament times. Throughout the Church's history there has always been a fascination with this fundamental question: who is Jesus? The fourth and fifth centuries, with their great Councils — Nicaea (325), first Constantinople (381), Ephesus (431), and Chalcedon (451) — have given the Christian community a basic language with which to deal with this question. Yet Christians continue to reflect, for the mystery of Jesus — which is the mystery of God among us — is a reality whose depths we can never plumb.

Personal Moments of Christological Awareness

Nor are these moments of Christological recognition and growth confined to the community of the Church as a whole. They also occur in the lives of each of us, as we move from hearing about Jesus to experiencing him in our lives, from learning about him in books or lectures to feeling his presence and activity in our lives. And there is not just one such moment: there are many as, through our lives, we move toward a deeper understanding of the answer we must give to the existential question: "Who do *you* say that I am?"

There is, then, a Church Christology and a personal Christology. These are not at odds with each other; rather they enrich each other. Yet is has to be said that neither will ever be adequate to express the depth of the Christological reality. Nor should we be distressed at the inadequacy of language. The important task is not so much to find words to express our experience — as Church or as individual person — as it is to respond to what the experience of the Lord calls us to.

A Final Note

Contemporary Christologies are often distinguished into Christology "from above" and Christology "from below." The first starts from the Word made flesh; the second begins with the Jesus of history. The Christology "from above" is about the preexistent Word of God who "comes down to earth," takes on human flesh, redeems us by dying on the cross and rising from the dead. Having accomplished our redemption, he returns to what had always been his exalted state at the right hand of the Father. Christology "from below" begins with Jesus who was born as a human being and is like us in all things except sin. Conscious of his mission from God, he proclaims the kingdom of God. He calls God "Abba" and invites people to believe in a God who loves and saves. The understanding of God that he preached was unacceptable to the religious leaders of his time. They had him crucified by Roman authorities. God vindicated his preaching by raising him from the dead and making him Lord and Messiah.

It is important to understand that both these Christologies are an attempt to explain what Christians mean when they say that Jesus is both God and human. Each has its distinctive starting point and emphasis. The Christology that begins with the divinity has undoubtedly been the more traditional one. The "low" Christology (from below) is probably more in favor today. It is difficult to begin from divinity (as the high Christology does), since we do not know God. It is easier to begin from humanity (the "low" Christology) because we have experience of humanity. In saying this, of course, I reveal my own preference. Yet I think we need to say that, because we are dealing with mystery, neither Christology is completely satisfactory. Either of them is almost forced, by the limitations of human language, into positions it does not want to be in. If you choose one, you risk underplaying his humanity; if you choose the other, there is the risk of ignoring his divinity. The only way out is to admit our limitations, all the while confessing: "Jesus is Lord."

7. Disciple (*Mathetes*)

The notion of a disciple (or student) relating to a master is a common phenomenon in many religions. In Hinduism, for instance, a young person will attach himself to a master, chosen either by himself or by his parents, under whom he will study the Hindu scriptures. The purpose of this study is to prepare him to assume his responsibilities in Hindu society by entering upon the next stage of life: the role of the householder.

In many religions a disciple attaches himself to a master in order to learn from that master and, eventually, become a teacher himself. In Judaism, for instance, the rabbis had their disciples who studied with them and learned the Torah and its interpretations under their direction. Disciples were deeply devoted to their masters and would commit their rabbis' teachings to memory. Yet great though their devotion might be, they conceived their discipleship as a temporary stage in their lives. They hoped to learn the wisdom of the ages from their masters so that they could become masters in their own right.

Being a disciple of Jesus is presented in the New Testament, especially in the Gospels, as something radically different from discipleship in other religions. First of all, Jesus' disciples did not choose to follow him; the initiative was his: he chose them to be his followers. Whether you read the account of the vocation stories in the Synoptics (e.g., Mark 1:17) or in John (e.g., 1:43), it is always the same story: Jesus saying: "Follow me."

Secondly, the attachment of Jesus' disciples was not primarily to his teachings, but to his person. Whereas the disciples of a rabbi went to great pains to learn each of his teachings word for word so that they could repeat it from memory, there is no evidence that Jesus required this approach of his disciples. In fact, the evidence is to the contrary. The New Testament itself is the best witness of how little the disciples of Jesus were concerned with reporting word for word what he said. The Gospels as we have them are not verbal transmissions of what Jesus said; rather they are accounts of his life, passion, death, and resurrection. The disciples of Jesus were witnesses to the resurrection-event rather than mere channels of a verbal tradition. Their recollections of Jesus as a teacher were secondary to their proclamation of the decisive eschatological action that God had realized in him when God raised him from the dead. Interestingly, there is no indication that his words and teachings were any source of strength to them after his death. The Gospel evidence seems to say that his death appeared to cut off their tie with him. That is why after the resurrection there is a restoration of fellowship with him — a fellowship that had been broken by their failure to remain faithful to him. It is no accident that from the time of Gethsemane Luke does not use the word "disciple" again in this Gospel. He does not resume use of this term for followers of Jesus until the sixth chapter of Acts. Jesus' disciples are not so much bearers of a tradition as they are witnesses to the fact that God was in Jesus reconciling the world to Himself (see 2 Cor. 5:19). Jesus, who is their master, is never thought of as head of a school of thought; he is the living Lord. He is not just a proclaimer of truths; he is the Truth (see John 14:6).

A third difference about those called to be disciples of Jesus is that he claims the total allegiance of his disciples. Discipleship is permanent, not temporary. It is complete, not partial. It is a call that surely involves grace: "No one," he says, "can come to me unless the Father who sent me draws him" (John 6: 44, 65). It moves people to leave their boats, toll-office, and family. It is a discipleship that is costly.

So demanding is Jesus' call to discipleship that one must be prepared to abandon father and mother, son and daughter; indeed, one must be ready to lose his/her own life. One of the strongest statements of the cost of discipleship is to be found in Luke's Gospel (with parallels in Matthew and Mark) in the course of the ongoing instruction Jesus gives his disciples as he journeys toward Jerusalem, the city of destiny. Luke tells us:

> Now great multitudes accompanied him; and he turned and said to them: "If anyone comes to me and does not hate his [her] own father and mother and wife and children and brothers and sisters, yes, and even his [her] own life, he [she] cannot be my disciple" (14:25–26).

This is the Revised Standard translation of this text. The New American Bible softens the harshness of the words a bit by substituting "turn one's back on" for "hate." It is helpful to know that the word that has been translated in these two different ways is the Greek word *miseo*. This Greek verb can be given a strong meaning or a weak meaning. To translate it as "turning one's back on something" is to give it its weakest meaning. Its strongest, and probably most literal, meaning is "to hate." (One might note, in passing, that the word "misogynist" is made up of the verb *miseo* and the noun *gyne*, which means woman; and a misogynist, by definition, is "one who hates women.")

I hope the reader will excuse this excursion into etymology, but I think it is important if we are to understand the truly radical character of the demand that Jesus makes on his disciples. What he is saying in this text is that there can be no such thing as half-hearted commitment. Half-hearted commitment is no commitment at all. He is demanding our complete allegiance. When the choice is there, we must choose him over any and all of the persons and things we most cherish in our lives. In interpreting this passage, it is important to realize that Jesus is doing two things. First, he is enunciating a principle. Then, in a powerfully dramatic picture, he offers an example to illustrate the principle. A hasty reading of the passage could make the mistake of turning the example into a principle and this is not intended at all.

The principle Jesus is enunciating is the fundamental principle of Christian discipleship: following Jesus must take priority over everything else in our lives. This means that we must be prepared to sacrifice anything, no matter how precious it may be, that would prevent this total commitment to him. This is the principle. His words about father and mother and relatives are offered as an example of realities that are very precious to us. Jesus is not saying that family ties are, of themselves, an obstacle to true discipleship, or even that they will often be such an obstacle. He is simply saying that however much we love our families (and Jesus himself spoke, on other occasions, about the obligation we have to love father and mother and brothers and sisters), we must reserve first place in our lives for him. And in the unlikely event that family ties do interfere with his prior claims to our loyalty, then he makes it clear that we must choose him. It should be evident, however, that he is not saying that this is the choice most of us have to make: either Jesus or our family. Actually, the things in our lives that threaten our total allegiance to him may well be much more subtle. They are more likely to be things in our own selves that hold us back.

To be disciples of Jesus is to be called to be like him who came among people not to be served, but to serve. The only greatness that he is willing to recognize is that which is ours when we become like children in total dependence on our Father and are willing to be the servants of one another and of all. This is especially true of those who have authority among the disciples: they must not "lord it over others"; rather they must be the servants of all. The identifying mark of disciples of Jesus will be the love they have for one another. His personal command to them was and is: "Love one another, as I have loved you" (John 15:12).

The word used in the Gospels for disciples is the Greek *mathetes*. It is used more than 250 times in the Gospels and Acts (though nowhere else in the New Testament). There is a certain ambiguity as to who are being referred to when this word is used. It is wrong to equate the term simply with the Twelve who are clearly a symbolic representation of the twelve tribes of Israel and, therefore, of the people of God. "Disciple" clearly extends to a much larger group. It has been suggested that the followers of Jesus might be seen as three groups in concentric circles around him. The innermost circle would be the Twelve, next would be the disciples, then there would be those who could be called simply "followers" or believers. What is important to realize is that all are called to a radical commitment to Jesus. These three circles may indicate different degrees of personal involvement with him, but the same call to total allegiance is addressed to all. There are no second-class citizens among those called to follow Jesus. All are called to give all.

6

The Third Rung: *Oratio*

We have spoken about the Word of God: how we let it *happen* to us (*lectio*) and how we let it shape the way we think about our lives and our actions (*meditatio*). We have also had a brief interlude about some key texts of Scripture and some basic theological themes that have developed out of Scripture. Now it is time for us to being to think about what the Word of God moves us to do. There may be times when we shall have to say that there doesn't seem to be anything in particular that the Word of God is moving us to do. We may perhaps feel that nothing really happened to us as we read and reflected. In such instances, we have to be patient and wait. We have to come back to the Scriptures later, and perhaps further reading will show us the direction in which we ought to be moving. That does not mean that our reading and reflection have been worthless, but only that the Word of God needs to penetrate more deeply into our hearts. It may be that our reading was more on the surface than we thought. It could even be that we did not really want to experience what the Word was calling us to. There are times when our hearts are hardened, and we may not even realize it. It takes time for God's Word to reach us and to soften soil that, perhaps unwittingly, has become hard.

Most frequently it will probably be true that our reading and reflection will move us to respond to God. Sometimes the Word of God will overwhelm us and the need to respond to God will seem quite irresistible. God's Word becomes a compelling Word. One way of putting what happens to us, when we read and reflect on the Scriptures, is to say that we fall into the hands of God, somewhat as the man on the way to Jericho fell in among robbers. Now I know that it isn't very polite and maybe not very good theology to compare God to a robber. I do want to say though that a comparison of this kind is not altogether indefensible. After all, our language about God is metaphorical, and there are times when seemingly odd metaphors may help us to capture something of the truth about God that "standard" ones don't. So there may be ways in which the comparison I am suggesting might offer some helpful insight. The man who fell among robbers was stripped — stripped of everything he had that was worthwhile. Maybe it isn't too fanciful to think that when we expose ourselves to the Scriptures we fall into God's hands and we are stripped too, not of anything in us that is worthwhile, but — quite the contrary — of those things in us that we knew we ought to get rid of, but hadn't really faced up to until the Scripture we read caught our eyes and dug into our hearts and began to do a bit of burning there.

I don't want to belabor the point, but in defense of the comparison I have suggested, I want to quote a quite significant text from the Epistle to the Hebrews. The unknown author of this book has something rather striking to say about "falling into God's hands." "It is a fearful thing," he says, "to fall into the hands of the living God" (10:31). Now I have to admit that he is talking here about God's judgment, but that is all right if we think of judgment as facing a critical decision in our lives that God forces us to look at. *Krisis*, from which the words "crisis" and "critical" come, is a Greek word that means judgment. And falling into the hands of God is certainly a call to make a judgment about our lives.

If one looks carefully at this text from Hebrews, it may

become clearer that my comparing the "falling into the hands" of God which Scripture brings about, with the plight of the man on the Jericho road, who fell among robbers, is not as fanciful as one might suppose. At least it is worth pointing out that Luke uses the same Greek verb in his parable as is used by the author of the Hebrews (namely the verb *empipto*). Both are talking about "falling into someone's hands."

In fact, it might not take us too far afield to note that in classical Greek the word *empipto* can have a positive meaning: it can refer to a friendly "falling in with" someone. It can mean linking up with someone, joining him/her in a common venture. I don't want to stretch the word too far, but as a very final point, I might recall that we do use the expression "falling in love" with someone. That too when it truly happens is a kind of stripping: we are stripped of our selfishness and let another become the center of our lives.

What I am suggesting, then, is that what happens to us when we read Scripture and reflect on it is that we "fall into the hands of God." And, whether or not I am stretching unduly a Greek word used in Scripture, I want to say that this falling into the hands of God means a number of things—things of course that happen, generally, over a long period of time. First, there is a purification that takes away some of the things that prevent us from giving our hearts and minds wholly to God (this is like falling in among robbers and being "stripped," but having it done as it were in reverse: losing what is worthless rather than what is worthwhile). But also, secondly, "falling into the hands of God" means falling in with Him and with His plans; it means making common cause with Him in the great venture of "making the kingdom come." Thirdly and finally, I want to let falling into the hands of God mean: "falling in love with Him," in such a way that He becomes in our thinking and living what He is in reality: the center of all that is and, more specifically, the center of who we are.

Meaning of Prayer

"Being in the clutches of God," as I have just tried to clarify it, means in its deepest dimension a profound experience of our creaturehood. In relation to God this betokens a realization of our total dependence on Him. In relation to others of His creatures the experience of creaturehood leads us to an understanding of our interdependence with all of them. In a word, reading and reflecting on Scripture enables us to see that we need God—without whom we would not be—and that we need one another, for we are related to one another in interlocking relationships that link our lives and activities together irrevocably.

This sense of dependence on Him and interdependence with our brothers and sisters can lead us to many things. One of them is prayer (*oratio*). By prayer here I mean what I have described briefly in chapter 2 as "the prayer of the choir." The "prayer of the choir" is the way in which we acknowledge in ritual the ontological fact of this dependence and interdependence. When I speak of "ritual" here, I am using it in the primal sense of the need experienced by all human persons to express in actions and words, significant to them, the sentiments of dependence and interdependence that are deep in their psyche. And, as I have already pointed out in chapter 2, by "prayer of the choir" I am referring to a particular ritual of prayer in sung words that is performed in choir but which may also be meaningfully performed with words, but probably not sung words, by an individual person apart from any relationship to a choir. I use the phrase "prayer of the choir" simply to indicate that the choir does preeminently what we all need to do in expressing our sense of dependence and interdependence.

Oratio and *Operatio*

The purpose of this chapter is to continue "climbing" the rungs of Guigo's ladder and to discuss the third rung, prayer (*oratio*), to which Scripture may move us: prayer that expresses our need of God and our need for one another. I would not, however, want to leave the impression that the only concern that emerges from Scripture is to get us to pray. When we read the Word of God with openness of mind and heart, it also calls us to action in this world: action for the building up of the kingdom of God and action that fosters the well-being, physical as well as spiritual, temporal as well as eternal, of our sisters and brothers. I want to reserve for a later chapter, however, this call to engagement in the work of the kingdom and in the service of our fellow-men and women and devote this chapter to prayer.

The theme I hope to develop is that all prayer in one way or another is the articulation of our dependence (on God) and our interdependence (with one another).

Dependence

I have already discussed our relationship to God in terms of our utter dependence on Him in chapter 2, and the reader might want to return there and reread that section. We are accustomed to use the term "dependence" in a number of contexts that are not necessarily religious. Thus we may say to a friend who has agreed to say a good word for us so that we may get a job: "I'm depending on you." There are many situations of dependence in our experience. Children depend on their parents for fundamental necessities of life. Students depend on their teachers to give them guidance along the path of learning. People who are sick depend on nurses and doctors to help them get well. In each of these instances dependence is partial or it is a dependence wherein someone else could be substituted for the one on whom one depends.

When we use the word "dependence" in a religious context — to speak of our dependence on God — we are in a completely different realm of experience. It is as if the word "dependence" in this context means so much more that it can almost be said to mean something that is in fundamental ways different. Our dependence on God is not partial but total—so total that without Him we would simply cease to be. And no one can substitute for Him. The word "dependence" derives from the Latin word *pendere*, which literally means "to hang." *Dependere* would mean "to hang on to something or someone." We can think, for instance, of a little girl crossing the street and hanging on to her mother's hand. If they are jostled in a large crowd crossing the street and become separated, it may be a frightening experience for the child; but she will probably make it to the other side of the street, even if the going is somewhat precarious. Again the analogy limps badly, for the child is able to go on even when she becomes separated from her mother, whereas if we let go of God, or rather if God lets go of us, we cannot go on being at all. The analogy would be more appropriate if we could imagine a situation in which, if the mother let go of her child's hand, the child would simply vanish into thin air. This would not happen, for the child is a distinct person whose being is not dependent on her mother. Perhaps I am overemphasizing something that is quite clear to the reader. If I am, I hope my eagerness to clarify the meaning of "dependence" will be accepted as proof of the radical importance I want to give to this notion. There can be no real understanding of prayer unless the meaning of "dependence," with the subtleties it involves, is appreciated and, to some degree at least, experienced.

The Prayer of Praise and Thanks

When we begin to realize that, save for God, we hover on the brink of nothingness, then surely we begin to pray. And in the first instance, our prayer is *praise*. We are moved to shout *hallelujah*, which is a cultic cry of praise. *Hallelujah*, deriving from the Hebrew *halah* plus *yah*, the abbreviated form of the divine name, means a number of things: admiration, adulation, together with the rejoicing that accompany these: all of which can be expressed in the word "praise."

Probably the earliest cries of *hallelujah* in Israel did not come from an appreciation that the Lord God was the source of existence for each individual Israelite; rather Israel began to praise God because of what He had done for His people. Summing up what He did was the Exodus event whereby He delivered them from slavery. Then there were other events in their history in which they saw the hand of their God and praised Him. Worth noting is that even when their God seems to be punishing them for their infidelities, they still praise Him for all He has done for them. Nowhere are the praises of God sung more beautifully and more extravagantly than in the prayer-book of God's people, the Psalter. It is not until we get into the Psalms from the period of the exile and after that the sweet singers of Israel begin to speak, not only of God's deeds in history, but also of His deeds before history began. In the later Psalms God is praised as Creator as well as Savior. This represents a movement toward a more sophisticated understanding of God: a realization that the God whom they came to know in the very beginning of their history is not just the God who saves them. He is also the God who brings them into existence. His first act of "saving" them was delivering them not from the hands of their enemies, but from the depths of their nothingness. There is a movement toward knowing that without Him they were not simply powerless, they were nonexistent.

Praise of God is often indistinguishable from gratitude. Yet it is worth noting that in the Scriptures, especially in the Psalms, the motif of thanking God is not nearly so prominent as praising Him. The normal biblical stance in the face of God's mercy, love, and graciousness is not to thank Him but to praise Him.

There is a difference between praise and thanks. Suppose you do a favor for me. The normal thing for me to do would be to thank you in whatever way was appropriate and let it go at that. The biblical perspective would say: it is good for you to *thank* your friend, but it would be better if you *praised* him. How would praise differ from thanks? Praise would mean telling others of the favor you have done for me. Thus thanks requires only two parties: a benefactor and the one who benefits. Praise, however, requires not just two parties but three. In addition to the benefactor and the one who benefits, there must be an audience: namely, someone or some group I must impress by telling them enthusiastically about the favor you have done for me.

One of the difficulties we experience in the celebration of liturgy is that liturgical prayer is first and foremost praise, and we are more comfortable with thanking than with praising. "Thanking" is usually a quieter and more restrained expression of emotion, while "praise" calls for more enthusiasm and excitement than we generally are able to muster. As "sophisticated" people we tend to express gratitude rather than praise. It is an interesting psychological phenomenon that the opposite attitude seems to prevail among children. They are notoriously slow in learning to say thank you; they have to be taught to say it and often it takes time and patience. But praise comes quite spontaneously to them. They may forget to thank their Aunt Maggies for the birthday gifts, but they go out among their friends and want to tell anyone who will listen about the wonderful gifts that the Aunt Maggies gave them. They may forget to thank their Dad for teaching them how to throw a curve ball, but they will boast to their friends what a great pitcher their father is.

My intent is not to denigrate the value of gratitude as a sentiment to be expressed in prayer, but simply to suggest that biblical and liturgical prayer seem to set a higher premium on the prayer of praise. Perhaps this suggests, since praise requires at least in intention if not in reality a third party, that it is not only appropriate but also very beneficial to prayer that we pray with others when this is possible. Jesus said: "Where two or three are gathered in my name, there am I in the midst of them" (Matt. 18:20). It is very heartening to see that more and more small groups of Christians are gathering together to pray

and to support one another in prayer. Certainly the Lord Jesus
is in our midst when we gather for worship on the Lord's Day,
though the sense of presence varies widely in a large congrega-
tion of people. Without wanting to take anything away from the
importance of the Sunday worship and the experience of presence there, it is nonetheless worth noting that Jesus spoke of
two or three, not of two or three hundred. Obviously the larger
community of the local Church and the small group coming
together for mutual support must not be set over against one
another. They complement each other. Each has its proper
importance.

The Prayer of Repentance

I mentioned earlier that in the biblical perspective, Israel even
praised God for His graciousness in punishing them so as to
bring them to repentance. Another aspect of prayer, then, is
repentance for failures, faults, and sinfulness, a repentance that
seeks and leads to reconciliation. Repentance is one of those
biblical words that is of key importance. The reader might want
to refer back to the discussion of repentance (*metanoia*) in chapter 5. Here I would like to discuss it as prayer that leads to
reconciliation.

Our prayer of repentance is concerned, first of all, with our
sinfulness. There are a number of ways of reflecting on our
sinfulness, not all of them profitable. A useful approach perhaps is to realize that there are sins of malice and sins of
weakness. It is the second category and not the first, I think,
that is our most important problem. Normally, we are not
malicious persons. Indeed, even the sins we commit that seem
to be sins of malice are most likely to be, at bottom, sins that
flow from our weaknesses. We know Christ's command of love.
We are very conscious that we should love the Lord our God
with all our hearts and that we should love our neighbors as
ourselves. We really want to fulfill the command of love; but we

are weak and we often falter in the face of the divine command. We are like Peter in the passion narratives of the Gospels: strong in protestations of love, but often ever so weak in carrying them out. Think of Peter in the courtyard of the high priest's palace during the trial of Jesus. Here is the man who at the Supper had protested his undying loyalty to Jesus, the man who had drawn his sword in the garden to protect Jesus; but suddenly he is a weakling, scared for his life, cringing at the casual words of a servant girl, denying that he even knows Jesus. And all the while he is saying, "I don't know the man," his love for Jesus is like a lump in his throat.

Peter finally turns away, not from Jesus, but from the scene of his weakness. He goes out and weeps bitterly. Surely there is no malice here, no serious sin. There is only pitiful weakness. Peter wants to say with all his heart: "Of course I know him. I am one of his followers. I am ready to die with him." But, alas, all the bravado is gone. Peter flees for his life. How pathetic he appears in this very real denial of Jesus. Yet we must not forget this is the same Peter who had professed: "You are the Christ." This is the Peter who will later say, with a confidence that not even his denial could shake: "Lord, you know that I love you."

A legend exists which says that all his life Peter wept over his denial — so much so that his weeping dug furrows in his cheeks. This legend, I suggest, is false to the Gospel. As he rushed away from that courtyard, Peter knew that he was already forgiven. After all, could he forget that he had once asked: "How often should I forgive — until seven times?" and had been told: "Not seven times but seventy times seven times." Could Peter possibly doubt that he was forgiven? No question: he was conscious of his guilt, filled with shame for his failure. But he was more conscious of the Lord's forgiveness. That is why when the risen Jesus asked him: "Do you love me?," he can say, with a confidence born not of his own strength, but of God's mercy: "Lord, you know that I love you."

How like Peter we tend to be — sinning not because we are

strong in our proneness to evil, but because at times we are weak in our commitment to the Gospel. We want to love, forgive, serve, but at times we are weak and we fail. But then what often happens is that we become discouraged. We begin to question God's love for us not because we think He is unloving, but because we think we are unlovable. So many Christians, who ought to know better but maybe have been taught poorly, cringe before God because they think of Him as one who punishes. Such a god is no more than an idol: a projection of our own need to feel worthy coupled with the uneasy feeling that we are in fact unworthy. We look for goodness in ourselves that might move God to love us, and failing to find it, we fear Him as a God who needs to see goodness in us and who in the clarity of His vision sees only evil.

One of the keys to the reconciliation we seek in our prayer of repentance is the shattering realization that, no matter how hateful we may appear to ourselves, we are not hateful to God. Realizing this helps us to see the difference between our love and His. Our love is a need; His a gift. We need to see goodness in ourselves in order to love ourselves, whereas He does not. For ultimately, He loves us not so much because we are good but because He is. The root of true love is not so much the will to love, but the *faith* that we are loved by God, irrespective of any worth we can prove. Thomas Merton once wrote to a correspondent:

> You say you don't think you love God and that is probably perfectly true. But what matters is that God loves you, isn't it? If we had to rely on *our* love, where would we be? (*The Hidden Ground of Love*, p. 375)

When we pray the prayer of repentance, then we do indeed need to think of our sins, but never out of context. And the context is love: first, our love, the efforts we make to love God and one another (faltering efforts at times perhaps, but nonetheless genuine) and, secondly and most importantly, God's undefeated and undefeatable love for us.

Levels of Reconciliation

Reconciliation, which is the goal of our prayer of repentance, can be seen at a number of levels. First, there is inner reconciliation, in which we seek to acquire a measure of harmony and unity in our sometimes shattered, alienated hearts. But there is also reconciliation at the vertical level—between ourselves and God, and at the horizontal level—between ourselves and our sisters and brothers. Finally, there is an aspect of reconciliation that we perhaps do not think of often enough: reconciliation in the various structures that so strongly influence our lives and the cultural milieu in which we live. True repentance requires, in other words, that we come to grips with the institutional realities in our lives and with the corporate dimension of sin.

Corporate Sinfulness

Corporate sinfulness is difficult to define; it is so complicated and involves the complicity of so many different people. Yet, if we are truly saying the prayer of repentance, we must assume our share of responsibility for the corporate sinfulness that exists in the structures that, for good or for ill, influence people's lives in our day. There are, among others, two huge structures to which we belong: our nation and our Church. Both ought to be centers of freedom and community. At times, however, either or both of them can become places of oppression and alienation. We have no right to treat our nation or our Church as if it were something "out there": something outside of us for which we are not accountable. We have to accept our share of responsibility for the policies of our nation and our Church.

We cannot shoulder this kind of responsibility alone. That is why it is important that as God's people we become true communities and not just aggregates of people. It is in community that we hear the voice of the Spirit calling us to responsibility and giving us the courage to act as God's people: a people who are not afraid to confront and identify sinfulness, oppression, and unfreedom in our midst. As God's people we especially have to assume accountability for the corporate sinfulness that may exist in the Church, realizing that any suppression of legitimate freedom makes the Church less credible and less truly a sign in the world of the kingdom of God. It is only as free sons and daughters of God that we can attain our full stature of maturity in Christ. While we are on the way toward that maturity, we need to pray the prayer of repentance for whatever may be a barrier along that way.

It can perhaps be seen how the prayer of repentance is akin to the prayer of praise and thanksgiving. In the latter we look back to God's gracious deeds on our behalf; in repentance we look forward to His forgiveness and His healing touch that will make us whole. Always the motive of our prayer is the graciousness of our God. Praising, thanking, repenting are different forms of counting the ways He loves us. They are also different ways of proclaiming our total dependence on Him.

Intercessory Prayer
There is another form of prayer—which for some people is probably the only form they think of when they think of prayer—and that is the prayer of petition or intercessory prayer. Intercessory prayer, so it seems to me at least, is a great mystery. When we pray the other forms of prayer we know exactly what we are doing and why; we also have a reasonably clear notion of what we intend should emerge from this kind of prayer.

Intercessory prayer, on the other hand, is surrounded by ambiguities that inevitably call forth a number of questions. The crassest question of all, of course, is: does it work? But there are other questions, slightly less utilitarian in character. What are we intending to achieve when we offer petitions to God? Are we endeavoring to clue God in on matters He may have overlooked? Are we trying to get something or someone changed; and if so, what or whom do we have in mind: the circumstances in which we are, ourselves, someone else, God? Is it a proper thing for us to petition God? Or would we be better off just letting God "run" things, without our offering suggestions for improving the way things operate? What do we really expect as a result of our petition? Is offering a petition to God somewhat like buying a ticket in a lottery: we don't really expect any return, but it doesn't require any great effort on our part; so why not take the chance that something good may come?

There is mystery in intercessory prayer, not only because it poses a number of questions that are not easily answered, but also because it touches on other mysteries that somehow are intertwined with any answers we give to the questions posed above. There is the mystery of God's nature and activity (e.g., His creating and sustaining things in being), the mystery of a universe whose creation is pictured in Genesis as a transformation of chaos into order and which seems continually on the brink of falling back into its original chaos, the elusive mystery of our free will and what it may mean in relation to our total dependence on God and the interdependence we have with one another.

Thus, intercessory prayer forces us to ask a number of questions, some quite profound, others more easily grasped; it also sets us tripping on the heels of a number of mysteries that will always elude our comprehension. The fact that there are questions to face and mysteries to grapple with does not mean we should give up talking about intercessory prayer. It does mean, however, that after we have shed all the light on it that we can, we must be ready to live with the darkness that will still remain.

After all, mysteries are not problems to be solved: they are realities to be lived with. The fact that we can never know everything about them does not mean that what we can know is not valuable.

There is a story in Genesis (chapter 18) that highlights some of the questions and the mysteries involved in petitionary prayer. It is the charming story of Abraham who bargains with God over the fate of the city of Sodom. It is a picturesque narrative of a man pleading with his God: it reads like a scene from a Middle East bazaar, as Abraham does his best to reduce to the lowest possible figure the number of good residents God will demand as a condition for sparing the city. A superficial reading of the story might suggest that Abraham was rather good at intercessory prayer: he nearly got God to change His mind. But in the end God prevails and—though the story does not make this explicit—presumably Abraham submits. (It is worth noting that the people of Islam, who like Jews and Christians trace their origins back to Abraham, call themselves "Muslims," which means "people who submit," and see Abraham as the model of those who "submit to God".)

As we read this story, we are moved to ask: Was Abraham's prayer answered or did God refuse his request? The obvious intent of his petitioning was to get God to change His mind, but did his prayer actually have a meaning that goes much deeper than that? Is the point of the story Abraham's submission to God rather than what it appears to be on the surface: his effort to manipulate God? Does the mysterious question that God is described as asking Himself, as He and Abraham travel toward Sodom: "Shall I hide from Abraham what I am about to do?," give us an insight into the meaning of this scene and an approach into the meaning of intercessory prayer? Was Abraham, through his petitions and because of the seriousness with which God takes him, gradually being brought to some kind of insight into what God was doing? Is this one of the important goals of intercessory prayer: to help us to see more clearly into the mystery of God's providence working in our lives?

Intercessory prayer is as old as religion itself. The earliest prayers we know from primitive religions are prayers in which people call on their god — whatever name they may give him or her — to supply what they need in their lives and are unable to achieve through their own resources. Some years ago I put together — for a Religion 101 course — a series of prayers of primitive peoples. The collection made it quite clear that what they prayed for to their gods were the common needs that all people have to face: deliverance from sickness, help on hunting expeditions, victory over their enemies in war.

This last is a very common petition and quite understandable among peoples who limited their concept of neighbor to those who belonged to their own tribe. The outsiders were their enemies and presumably the enemies of their god too. Hence they expected his/her help in battle. Indeed, so strong was this sense of their god's involvement in their battles that if they were defeated, the defeat created not only economic and social problems; it also created, at a deeper level, a religious crisis: why was their god not powerful enough to give them victory in battle?

One of the prayers I discovered for my collection was the prayer of an American Indian tribe who were about to go on a thieving expedition against a neighboring tribe. They prayed, asking their god to cast a deep sleep over the camp they were about to rob, so that their victims might not awaken and interfere with the success of their thieving expedition.

This quite extraordinary prayer points up a danger that always lurks in the shadows of intercessory prayer: the danger of turning it into magic or superstition. Magic is the effort to manipulate God: to use Him to get our needs satisfied. And we have to warn ourselves that even good Christians, on occasion at least, are not above this primitive instinct that turns religion (which means submission to God) into magic (which attempts to put God's power at the service of our concerns).

Yet, despite its inherent dangers, Jesus does not repudiate intercessory prayer. On the contrary, he encourages us to perseverance and persistence in interceding with God. We should note, however, that he puts this exhortation to continuous prayer in the context of a model of this kind of prayer that he offers us, in the prayer we have come to know as the "Lord's Prayer."

The "Lord's Prayer"

Reflecting on the Lord's Prayer can perhaps help us to see more deeply the meaning and purpose of intercessory prayer. For one thing there is nothing self-centered, self-seeking, or petty about the petitions of the Lord's Prayer. There is a proper priority and an acceptance of responsibilities (some not easy, like settling for receiving God's forgiveness only to the degree that we give forgiveness to our sisters and brothers). We come to realize too that one of the deepest meanings of intercessory prayer is to inform not God but ourselves of our needs. Prayer should give us a lively awareness of how much we need God at every moment of our lives. We express our needs aloud that we may experience how deep and basic they really are.

Expectations in Intercessory Prayer

What are we to expect from our prayers of petition? Perhaps more a change in ourselves than in the external circumstances that may have prompted our prayer. Such prayer can lead to better self-knowledge. It can also bring God's strength: to help us deal with life's problems—the problems that may have prompted our prayer in the first place. There is a helpful verse in Psalm 138 which suggests that the grace of God's strength may be, at the very least, one of the significant ways of describing the way God answers our prayers. To grasp the meaning of this verse, one needs to remember that the poetic rhythm of the

Psalms involves parallelism, which means that the second part of the verse repeats the meaning of the first, but in a different way. The first part of verse 2 of Psalm 138 says confidently of God: "When I called upon you, you answered me." The second part of this verse, which, remember, is intended to parallel the first part, says: "You built up strength within me." What the psalmist is telling us is that "having God answer" our prayers is the same as "having Him build up strength" in us.

There is a saying of Jesus in Matthew and Luke that makes the same point, though Luke's version is much more forceful. In both cases the saying points to an obvious parallel: between a human father and the heavenly Father. It's a "how much more" argument. Matthew is content to give the parallel and the contrast: "If you, with all your sins, know how to give your children what is good, *how much more* will your heavenly Father give *good things* to anyone who asks him" (7:11). Luke's text is identical with Matthew's, with one significant difference: "If you, with all your sins, know how to give your children good things, *how much more* will the heavenly Father give the *Holy Spirit* to those who ask him" (11:13). Matthew's "good things" have become in Luke the "Holy Spirit."

It may be that in Luke's rendering of this text we have reached the true depths of the meaning of intercessory prayer. We ask for what we need and this we must do. It is most natural to us, and Jesus has told us to do it. In return, God gives us the greatest gift of all, the *Donum Dei:* the gift of His Holy Spirit to guide, to direct, to console us. The Holy Spirit comes to us in different ways, always in terms of what our real need is — however rightly or wrongly we may have identified that need.

Praying for Others

One of the aspects of intercessory prayer we need to consider is prayer that we offer for others (whether living or dead). What does it mean for me to pray for another? How does my prayer relate to God and to the one for whom I pray? The problems linked with prayer on behalf of others may be highlighted in an often repeated story: the prayer of St. Monica for her son Augustine. The story of her prayers and tears for his conversion are movingly related in Augustine's *Confessions*. It is often used to illustrate the importance and the efficacy of intercessory prayer. The Gospel that is read on the Feast of St. Monica appears a most appropriate one: the story of the raising of the widow's son at Naim. There is an obvious parallel between these two stories. Like the woman of Naim, Monica is a widow. Her son Augustine died spiritually in his youth; then in his mature young manhood God raises him from spiritual death and restores him, spiritually alive, to his mother.

There is, however, one important parallel that is missing from the story. The widowed mother in the Gospel story makes no petition to Jesus to restore her son to life. Jesus is reported as performing a miracle that was unrequested; he acted out of the spontaneity of his concern and compassion. In the case of Monica, on the other hand, she pleaded with God for many years, with prayers and tears, that God bring her son back from spiritual death. Thus we have two stories — each about a young man brought back to life — but in the Gospel story there is no request on the part of the mother, whereas in the Augustine story there is much prayer from his mother.

This contrast forces us to ask the question: Did Monica's prayers ultimately make any difference? Would God have given the grace of new life to Augustine even if his mother had not prayed for him — as Jesus gave life to the widow's son of Naim without any request having been made by her? These questions are unanswerable, because they are part of one of the great mysteries of intercessory prayer: the interplay between our freedom and the all-powerful and undefeatable love of God. It would surely be wrong to think that God was indifferent to Augustine's conversion and was persuaded to give him that grace only because Monica asked. This would imply that

Monica loved her son more than God did — surely an unacceptable position, since we know that God's love for each of us is unbounded. Yet it would be equally wrong to say that Monica's prayers had nothing to do with Augustine's conversion. For it is part of the mystery of God's love to involve us in the salvation of one another. God who can act without us chooses to act both with us and through us. God, who could have created all things by Himself, invites the participation of the earth, the sea, and especially of the man and the woman in His creative work. The earth and the sea bring forth various types of living beings. The man and the woman share the dignity of being cocreators with God of human life and therefore in a wondrous way of human freedom. This insight does not resolve the mystery of intercessory prayer or clarify necessarily what that prayer means in a particular instance. But at least it does give us a focus on the mystery.

Interdependence
Intercessory prayer helps us to understand the deep unity we have with one another in God and the interdependence that flows from that unity. Since we all find our identity and uniqueness in God, we are not separate from one another — even though each of us is distinctly unique. Cicero's description of a friend can perhaps be adapted here, in a way he perhaps would not have meant it, to indicate the communion that exists among us. He calls a friend an *"alter idem."* A friend is both "other" and "same," or as I have expressed it, "distinct," but "not separate." Because we are all grounded in God and hence share communion with one another (we are a "communion of saints"), we have responsibilities toward one another. Intercessory prayer is one way of fulfilling part of our responsibilities. To pray for another (living or dead) is to embrace that person in our love and concern. There may be instances where that "embrace" may be all that we can do to fulfill the responsibility that

flows from our interdependence; and it will be enough. The clasped hand, the loving embrace often say so much more than words can ever convey. And that is what intercessory prayer is in many instances: the clasped hand and the gentle embrace.

Miracles: Should We Expect Them?

One of the questions that the prayer of intercession poses is: Should we expect miracles? An initial answer to the question might well be: Why not? Of course a more reflective answer might say that it all depends on what you mean by "miracle." The word "miracle" derives from the Latin "*miraculum*" and means literally "an event that causes wonder." Surely there are plenty of "wonders" that we experience every day: the beauty of a glorious sunset, the joy in the face of a devoted mother as she looks lovingly at the infant in her arms. A first view of Lake Louise in the Canadian Rockies or of the Matterhorn at Zermatt in Switzerland produces a deep sense of awe and wonder. We see wonders too in the aged who face the future with a happy tranquillity and in the suffering who grow in courage as illness enervates their physical strength. The universe of nature and of human persons is full of wonders, if we open our eyes and really "see."

It is true, however, that when people speak of "miracles," they are generally referring not to those wonders that are a part of nature and life but to events that somehow disrupt the harmony and direction of nature's normal course. Here we need to speak in a more guarded way. For we are talking about the very meaning of creation. When Genesis describes the creation of the universe in its initial two chapters, the picture that the writer clearly intends to give is that God puts order and harmony into what before had been chaos. Without denying the power of God, on occasion at least, to "rearrange" that order and harmony, one would probably have to say that to disrupt that order and harmony, at least on a regular basis, could well mean a return to primitive chaos. We know, for instance, that the pull of gravity is a part of the harmony of nature on earth (though, interestingly, not in space). If that pull of gravity were regularly suspended, our existence would surely be chaotic. If our car were suddenly and unexpectedly to take off for the stratosphere or our dinner for the ceiling, if the unexpected were to become the "normal," one would never know what to expect. Life would be thrown into disarray. To put it crudely: Must we not say that God "is stuck" with the order and harmony that He has put into His creation — "stuck" (though not unexceptionlessly) for our good?

I have tried to say a few things that can shed some light on the mystery of intercessory prayer. My intent was not to resolve what must remain a great mystery, but to offer some suggestions that could help us to live, more intelligently and less anxiously, with that mystery. I want to conclude what can only be considered preliminary words on this subject with an observation. The ultimate intelligibility of intercessory prayer is to be found not in itself, but in that kind of prayer that I have called the "prayer of the desert": that quiet, humble, wordless prayer — beyond concept, beyond thought, beyond feeling — that helps us to grow in our awareness of God. Without this deep awareness of His dynamic involvement in our lives, we will probably become overanxious about intercessory prayer. With this "prayer of the desert" as the heart of our spirituality, there will be a stability and a serenity in our lives. For we know that we are in Him, and so is all else. Ultimately, this is what really matters. When we are truly aware of God and His presence, all our perspectives are modified. For they are charged with His presence.

7

The Fourth and Highest Rung: *Contemplatio*

Thus far we have been "climbing" Guigo's ladder and have arrived at the fourth rung which is contemplation. In understanding contemplation it will be helpful to see how Guigo relates it to the other three steps. In chapter 10 of the Latin text (chapter 12 of the Image translation), Guigo, after having described the four rungs separately, attempts to show how they are joined and united with one another. In rather picturesque language (which is not captured in the English translation) Guigo seems almost to personify the rungs of the ladder, having one "send" us to the other—somewhat like a person, going to a department store in search of a particular article, might be "sent" from one department to another. Thus reading (which we discussed in chapter 3 as letting the Word of God "happen" to us) "sends" us (*mittit* is Guigo's word) to meditation. Meditation (which we talked about in chapter 4 as reflection on God's Word to let it be directive of our lives) "sends" us (once again, *mittit*) to *oratio*, prayer.

Interestingly, at this point, Guigo makes a rather abrupt change in his language. He does not have prayer "send" us to contemplation. For contemplation, while it is presented as one of the rungs of the ladder, is yet something quite different from the others; it is in a class by itself. It does not flow out of the other three, as they seem to "flow" out of one another. For the other three are concerned with the use of various senses and faculties associated with human knowing and feeling. But contemplation goes beyond all senses and faculties. Guigo, therefore, is content to say that when it "comes" (the word he uses is *adveniens*), it rewards the work of the other three. It should be noted that he does not say that it comes as a reward of the other three; but rather that when it does come (he leaves open the way of its coming) it may be seen as the crown and glory of the other steps.

Another way of putting this is to say that, while the first three rungs of the ladder (reading, meditation and prayer) offer, each in its own way, an experience of God, the experience is a mediated one: it comes through the medium of words, concepts, thoughts. The time comes when a person is no longer willing to be satisfied with anything but a direct experience of God. It is at this point that he/she must turn to contemplation. Contemplation moves us beyond words and concepts to a direct experience of God, insofar as this is possible in this life.

Reading, meditation and prayer are concerned with *doing*: what God does for us, what we do in response. Contemplation, on the other hand, is concerned with *being*. It is moving from knowing what God does, which is really knowledge *about* Him, to knowing who He *is*. More than that, it is *letting go* of actions on my part so that I may simply *be* in the presence of God. Contemplation is a deep awareness that I am in the presence of God. Since, as I have already pointed out in chapter 1, we are always in the presence of God (that is the very condition of our being at all), contemplation is not some new reality that I discover. It is simply achieving a deep awareness of what always has been and is true of me: namely, that I am in God, as everything that is, is in God.

It is for this reason that Thomas Merton, especially after his exposure to Zen, speaks of contemplation in terms of being "aware" and being "awake." In his *New Seeds of Contemplation*, published in 1962, he describes contemplation as our spiritual life "fully awake, fully active, fully aware that it is alive" (p. 1). A few paragraphs later, he goes on:

> . . . contemplation reaches out to the knowledge and even to the experience of the transcendent and inexpressible God. It knows God by seeming to touch Him. Or rather it knows Him as if it had been invisibly touched by Him . . . Touched by Him Who has no hands, but Who is pure Reality and the source of all that is real! Hence contemplation is a sudden gift of awareness, an awakening to the Real within all that is real. A vivid awareness of infinite Being at the roots of our own limited being. An awareness of our contingent reality as received, as a present from God, as a free gift of love. (p. 2)

Note carefully how many times Merton uses the word "awareness" or "being awake." And he is talking about an awareness of something that always *is*. This may well help us to understand why Guigo is not content to think of contemplation as just one more rung on the ladder of perfection. It is a rung on that ladder, but it is more than that. The other three — reading, meditation, prayer — are different things that a person may do if he/she wants to exercise spiritually, just as walking, running, jogging are different things a person may do if he/she wants to exercise physically. Contemplation is also an exercise that a spiritual person might want to engage in; but it is more than that. It is a way of being. That means that there is a difference between seeing contemplation as an exercise (like, say, meditation) that one might give a certain amount of time to and seeing it as a way of life. It would be a misunderstanding of the richness of the contemplative experience to say: "Now I am going to give an hour of my busy day to contemplation and for this hour I will be a contemplative." It would perhaps be more accurate to say: "I am a contemplative. Contemplation is a habitual stance in my life. Now I shall set aside an hour to intensify that ongoing experience."

For we are—all of us—contemplatives at the root of our being. At the root of our being we are one with God, one with each other, one with the world in which we live. Spending time in the silence of contemplation must not, therefore, be looked upon as a means of achieving this unity, but rather of recognizing that it is there. Silent contemplation does not make us contemplatives, but it can make us aware that we are truly contemplatives, though—it may well be—at a level of perception we do not often achieve. We need to be awakened to the contemplative dimension of our lives. It is there for the awakening. There is a Zen saying: "If you understand, things are just as they are; if you do not understand, things are just as they are." We are contemplatives at the core of our being. This is the way things are, whether we understand or not. But what a difference it makes when we do understand!

"Exercise" and Dimension of Life

Contemplation, therefore, may be seen as an "exercise" of the spiritual person; seen in this way, it is the last and the highest rung on Guigo's ladder. But it may also be thought of as a basic "dimension" of the human person. As an "exercise," it makes demands on our time; and it is important to spend time in silent contemplation, because we need to be "awakened." But as a basic "dimension" of all of us (our oneness with God and with people and with all that is) it is a reality that is always present, whether we are awakened to it or not. Contemplation is nothing more or less than being ourselves in *total awareness*. It is for this reason that I like to refer to the exercise of contemplation or contemplative prayer as the "prayer of awareness." It has also been called "centering prayer." And earlier in this book I referred to it as the "prayer of the desert."

Ordinary Awareness

One of the problems that hinders the flowering of the contemplative side of our being is the fact that, far from finding it easy to achieve this *total* awareness, we experience difficulty in arriving at ordinary, normal awareness of what belongs to our everyday experience. Oftentimes we do not really know *where we are*. We can walk in the midst of beauty — the flowers and trees in a garden, the shadows cast by the sun, the pillowy whiteness of clouds against blue sky — and we can miss it all. Often too we are not aware of *what we are doing*. We may, to all appearances, be reading a book, writing a paper, listening to a friend's conversation; but our thoughts may be miles away, as our minds wander to something we would prefer to be doing or something we shall be doing the next day. There are times too when we are not really aware of *why we are doing what we are doing*. We may be acting not out of choice, but simply yielding to the pressure of the crowd. We may think we are doing what we want, but deep down we know that we don't really want what we are doing.

One of the necessary preliminaries of achieving the total awareness that is the contemplative life is to come to ordinary awareness in our daily lives. We have to become *aware* of our relationships with other people: our families, our friends, the people we work with. We have to see the good that is in these relationships. For the good is what is there. The "bad" in a relationship is what is not there and what we wish were there. When we concentrate on what is not there, we fail to experience the good that is there. The same can be said of our work. There are certain elements we want to be there, but actually they are not. Again, if our whole attention is focused on what is not there, we miss the experience of the reality that is there.

This, of course, is not to suggest that we have to be content with what is there or that we should not try to better our relationships or improve our life-situation. But in the meantime we have to be truly and vitally aware of the good that does exist in our lives.

Preconceptions

There are certain obstacles that prevent us from being *aware* of God, of other persons, of the whole of reality. One of these obstacles is *preconceptions*. So often we fail to see reality as it is, because we decide beforehand what we are going to see. What happens then is that we tend to see what we expect instead of what is there. If, for instance, you expect someone is going to be unresponsive to you, the likelihood is that you will experience unresponsiveness in that person. Perhaps in such a situation we should try to see that the person *is* responding to us, but in a way that we did not anticipate. Because we did not expect this kind of response, we may not see the response that is there.

Preconceptions about other people can so often be an obstacle to real awareness of them. We fail to see what can be loved in them because we are so taken up with what cannot be loved in them. We miss seeing what is there because we are so occupied with what is not there. We also have preconceptions of what the experience of God should be; and when we don't have *that* kind of experience, we may think we are not experiencing God — when we actually are, but not in the way we expected.

Psychological tests have proved that we often see what we expect rather than what is really there. A group of people were tested with a deck of cards. The test was a simple one: a card was turned over and people were asked to identify what card they saw. One of the cards turned over was a red six of spades. Most of the people identified it as either a black six of spades or a six of hearts rather than a red six of spades. They did not see what was there. They saw what they expected to see.

Preoccupation

Another obstacle to true awareness is *preoccupation*. When we are preoccupied, we are thinking about some past experience or looking forward — sometimes with joy, sometimes with fear — to some future experience; so that we are prevented from experiencing what is happening now. Preoccupation is another word for distraction. Distraction means being pulled — not so much in the wrong direction, but in different directions at the same time. It is a kind of fragmentation of our lives and activities. If we are distracted in our prayer or in our efforts to be silent, it is probably because we are living distracted lives. To expect to be without distraction in prayer when we are constantly being distracted in our daily lives is to expect the impossible. We can be recollected at prayer only if we are doing our best to live recollected lives.

Total Awareness

At this point I should make it clear that the kind of awareness I have been talking about (what I have called "ordinary" awareness) is only a preliminary condition for achieving that *total awareness* that is contemplation. Total awareness is more than simply being in touch with what is happening about us (though that is important). Total awareness is not just a matter of being more alert than others. It is nothing less than a whole new way of life whereby we move to an entirely different level of consciousness, in which we come to see God, ourselves, and all else that is in an entirely new light. We undergo a *metanoia*, a conversion (see chapter 5) that is not just a change in behavior but a transformation of consciousness. We enter into a new world in which we see reality as it actually is; or, to say the same thing in a different way, we return to the world in which we were intended to exist from the beginning.

Return to Paradise

This return to our beginning is fundamental to Thomas Merton's understanding of contemplation, as it is indeed a common notion in Western spirituality. Contemplation is nothing less than a return to the mythical Garden of Paradise. It is a way of overcoming original sin: that condition of alienation that has put us out of touch with what is most real. For original sin carries us out of the Garden and leads us into dwelling places of unreality in which we do not see things as they really are. We see separation where we should see unity, the surface of things where we should see their depths.

For the Garden, from which original sin expels us, was the place where perfect harmony reigned and where the man and the woman were fully in touch with reality: the reality of God, themselves, and the world of nature. They were one with God as they walked in the cool of the evening with Him who is All. They were one with each other, not even having clothes to serve as barriers to their communion. They needed no zoos to keep the animals in; for in the Garden "the wolf is the guest of the lamb, the leopard lies down with the kid, the cow and the bear are neighbors, and the lion eats hay like the ox" (see Isaiah 11:6-7).

The mythical Garden of Genesis — that place of origins where there is only harmony and no discord, where there is only unity and no separateness, where reality is experienced as it truly is — was the Garden of contemplation. Expulsion from the Garden was a fall into discord, separateness, and illusion. It was a fall from contemplation.

Original Sin: Fall from Contemplation

There is a bull's-eye irony in the Genesis narrative of the first sin. For it describes the fall of the primordial pair from the state of contemplation as the "opening of their eyes." The irony is that as soon as their eyes are opened, they are no longer able to see. They can no longer see God, because they hide from Him; they are no longer at-one-with Him. They cannot see them- selves, for they put on clothes to hide their naked openness to each other. Instead of celebrating their communion, they hurl accusations at each other. There is now competition, manipula- tion, even sexism in the Garden. And where once they had exercised dominion over the rest of nature (keeping all things in harmony), now nature, in the image of the snake, rebels against them; and the trees and the plants yield their fruits only after much toil and sweat from the man and the woman.

There is a touch of genius in this irony that describes their sin as the opening of their eyes. Once they acquired, through the eating of the tree of the knowledge of good and evil, a pair of discriminating eyes that can be attracted by good and evil, they have to leave the Garden. For the Garden is the place of *true vision* where, because one's vision is single, one is attracted by what alone is really attractive, namely, the good. To have the knowledge of good and evil, while losing the wisdom to understand the difference between them, is to forfeit one's right to reside in the Garden. For to be drawn toward evil as if it were good is to fail to see it as it is. It is to enter into realms of unreality and, therefore, necessarily to leave the Garden.

Their eyes were opened not to the real world that they had known in the Garden, but to the world of separateness and superficiality: the world that is experienced outside the Garden. Their consciousness having been thus deformed, they could no longer readily distinguish the real from the unreal. That is why the opening of their eyes was, paradoxically, a loss of vision. It is not that Paradise was a dream world from which they awakened when their eyes were opened. It is rather that Paradise was the real world and their eyes were opened into a world of illusion, a dream state from which humanity has ever since been trying to awake.

The Christian life is a long journey of *metanoia*, whereby we return to Paradise. To accomplish this return, the *metanoia* of good behavior is not enough. What is required is a *metanoia* that reaches to the very roots of our being, to our center, our heart: a *metanoia* that transforms a consciousness that has been deformed by sin. This transformation of consciousness, achieved slowly and at times arduously, is the movement toward achieving realization of our contemplative nature.

Achieving this contemplative dimension is the way out of the dream state that mistakes the unreal for the real. That is why Thomas Merton describes contemplation as "an awakening to the Real" (*New Seeds of Contemplation*, p. 3). It is "life fully awake . . . fully aware that it is alive." It is "a breakthrough to a new level of reality." It is "a living contact with the infinite Source of all being, a contact not only of minds and hearts . . . but a transcendent union of consciousness, in which man and God become, according to the expression of St. Paul, 'one Spirit.'" It is "an extreme intensification of conscious awareness." "We are called," he tells us, "to become fully real . . . by attaining to a reality beyond the limitations of selfishness, in the Spirit" (ibid., p. 1). We are, in other words, called to return to Paradise.

Chuang Tzu's Dream

Other religions have grappled with different levels of consciousness and their relationship to the achieving of personal identity. Chuang Tzu, the eminent Taoist philosopher whom Merton admired so much, brings the problem to focus by telling of a dream he had one day:

> I, Chuang Tzu, dreamed I was a butterfly fluttering hither and thither, to all intents and purposes a butterfly . . . Suddenly I awakened . . . Now I do not know whether I was then a man dreaming that I was a butterfly or whether I am now a butterfly dreaming that I am a man.

Chuang Tzu's reflection of his experience is not as odd as on first hearing it might seem to be. The question he is posing is an important one: namely, what is the state of consciousness that puts me in touch with what is truly real?

We all recognize the difference between dream consciousness and ordinary waking consciousness. Suppose that I had a dream last night: I was standing on the edge of a very high cliff, looking down at huge jagged rocks hundreds of feet below. Suddenly, to my horror, the ground begins to give way beneath me, and I feel myself plunging headlong toward those jagged rocks.

In the middle of the fall I wake from my dream — perhaps with a cry of terror. As I arrive at ordinary waking consciousness, I experience a deep sense of relief when I realize that what seemed to be happening to me was not happening after all. It was only a dream. I had not been falling. There was no cliff. There were no jagged rocks.

What had happened to change such terror into peaceful relief? It was the fact that I had moved from one state of consciousness into another. While I was in the dream state, the dream objects were very real to me. It was only when I awakened that I realized that the dream objects had no substance. When I passed from the dream state to the state of ordinary waking consciousness, I was able to repudiate the dream objects.

Contemplation as a Basic Dimension of Life

Against the background of Chuang Tzu's dream and my own imagined "dream," I would like to invite the reader to reflect on a few possibilities. First of all, let us suppose that I were to enter into a dream state and never wake up from the dream. What would my situation be? Simply this: I would continue to experience the dream objects as if they were real. I would never repudiate them. For in order to do so, it would be necessary for me to move to another level of consciousness — namely, the state of ordinary waking consciousness.

But let me ask you to think of a further possibility. Suppose that the state of being awake, as we ordinarily conceive it, is not the state of a truly awakened consciousness after all? Suppose that there is a level of consciousness beyond our ordinary state of being awake, which—if you were to enter it—would give you a completely new and exciting experience of reality? This new experience would enable you to see that the objects of ordinary waking consciousness—which for so long a time you took to be real—are actually as illusory as the objects of a dream. Once you awakened to this new state of heightened consciousness, you would repudiate the objects of ordinary waking consciousness as not being real in any ultimate sense. In repudiating them, you would at last be fully awake, fully in touch with what is truly real. You would, as they say in Zen, have recovered your original face, or—in Christian terms—you would be back in Paradise. You would be seeing the "Face of the Invisible." You would at last have become the contemplative you were always meant to be, or rather the contemplative you always were, though up to then you hadn't known it.

The recovery of the contemplative dimension of our lives, therefore, goes far beyond a change in behavior. It is nothing less than a spiritual revolution that awakens deep levels of consciousness in us: not just the surface consciousness of our superficial self, but the inner depth consciousness of our real self, which we experience as nothing apart from the Being of God. It is what the Fathers of the Church, especially the Eastern Fathers, like to call the discovery of the heart: the heart, not as a physical organ, but as the center of my being, the place where I am most truly myself, the place where I experience God, the place where I find my brothers and sisters in an entirely new way.

Because we are contemplatives in the very core of our being, this return to the center—when finally we achieve it or even when we experience it only imperfectly—is never a complete surprise. As Merton says, "when we first taste the joys of contemplation, it strikes us as utterly new and strangely familiar . . . Although we had an entirely different notion of what it would be like, it turns out to be just what you seem to have known all along that it ought to be . . . We enter into a region which we had never even suspected, and yet it is this new world which seems familiar and obvious." (*New Seeds of Contemplation*, pp. 144–45). If I may put it in a paradox: in contemplation we *return* to a place where we have never been.

Contemplation and Community

Contemplation is an experience in solitude but not in isolation. For when I discover my center, my heart, and find God and my real self, I also find at that center my sisters and brothers and the deep communion I have with them. In a talk he gave at Calcutta, just a few weeks before he died, Merton spoke about this communion:

> It is beyond words and it is beyond speech and it is beyond concept. Not that we discover a new unity. We discover an older unity. My dear brothers, we are already one. But we imagine that we are not. And what we have to recover is our original unity. What we have to be is what we are. (*Asian Journal*, p. 308)

When at last we reach this level of transformed consciousness, we experience an intuition of the unity of all reality that carries us far beyond the surface dualism that normally characterizes our superficial consciousness. Life takes on a unity, a simplicity and a depth that, without contemplation, we would never know. We find our heart, our own inner truth. And we find it in God. We find too our sisters and brothers; and we find them in God.

Contemplation as the Fourth Rung of Guigo's Ladder

We have been talking about what it means to recover the contemplative dimension of our being: to know what it means experientially that in the depths of our being we are and always were "contemplatives." Yet coming to this experience does not happen just by the willing of it. There is much that we need to do (and, as I shall point out—what may be even more important—much we must *not* do) to dispose ourselves for this deep realization of who we are at the very core of our being. One of the things we need to do is to spend time regularly in that exercise of the spiritual person that Guigo calls "contemplation," and which he envisions as the highest of the rungs on the ladder we must climb if we are to actualize our potential as spiritual persons. As I have indicated earlier, this "rung" of the ladder of "spiritual exercise" can be called "the prayer of awareness," or "centering prayer," or "prayer of the desert." I shall, throughout the remainder of this chapter, simply refer to it as "contemplation." It should be understood that I am using it now not so much to designate that "total awareness" which is the contemplative dimension realizable in the human person, but as a specific "exercise" calculated to help awaken us to such total awareness.

Contemplation as Exercise

Contemplation in this sense is prayer that, in silence and generally in solitude, moves one beyond words, thoughts, and concepts to a direct experience of the presence of God insofar as this is possible in this life. Contemplation is being in the presence of God and letting go of thoughts, images, desires, concerns, anxieties. I let go of all that is not God so that I can truly experience the presence of God. And the final letting go, which removes the last veil that separates me from God, is letting go of "the self that lets go."

For someone who is in earnest about realizing his/her contemplative nature, it is—so I believe at least—essential that he/she spend some time each day in this "exercise" of contemplation. I believe that a person will find that twenty minutes (at least) of contemplative prayer in the morning and twenty minutes in the afternoon or evening will prove extremely beneficial. This of course is a general suggestion. Everyone will have to decide what is most appropriate for his/her life situation. I offer this suggestion, first, because I know it to be helpful and, secondly, because I want to underscore the seriousness of a daily commitment to contemplation for those who seek this way of deepening their union with God.

What should you do during the twenty minutes? The answer that most immediately comes to mind is: preferably, nothing. The point of this prayer is simply to *be* in the presence of God, not to *do* something in His presence. I should point out that *being* in the presence of God is not the same thing as *thinking about being* in the presence of God. To *think* of myself as being in God or to *think* of God as being in me is just as much *doing* something as the thinking about more obvious distractions is doing something. The prayer of awareness calls for a total abandonment of thinking. I must not think. I must not even try not to think. For to try not to think is to have one's mind on nonthinking; it is therefore a form of thinking, namely, thinking about not thinking.

Contemplation is being aware of God, but not self-consciously. I must not be watching myself to see if I am being aware of God. For then I am more aware of myself than of God. A musician who is conscious of herself singing will probably not sing well. She will be thinking about herself singing rather than losing herself in the music. If I think of God as an object that I as a subject am being aware of, then I have set myself apart from God. My awareness must be simple awareness or, if you prefer, simple awareness of God. But "I" as a subject of awareness must disappear. For the "I" that conceives of itself as the *subject* of the contemplative experience is the false self that as Merton says is destined to disappear like smoke up a chimney.

What is important is simply to be. I am most fully aware that I am in God when I am simply *being* myself: and being myself without doing, without even doing any reflection on what it is to be. In the production-oriented culture we live in, we are not good at doing nothing. Just being seems difficult precisely because instinctively we feel that we ought to be usefully involved with something or other.

Just being means letting go of the things that are in our minds and our hearts: our thoughts, our plans, our desires, our concerns, our anxieties. This is difficult for us for a number of reasons. First of all, our minds are "going" all the time—like a watch that is kept going simply by the motion of the hand without having to be wound up. We don't have to be wound up either; we are so deluged with thoughts and feelings that we are scarcely aware of their diversity or, sometimes, even of their presence. Moreover, one of the problems involved in letting go of activity, even for a brief moment of prayer, is that it may seem to pose a threat to our identity. The Cartesian *"Cogito, ergo sum,"* that has so strongly influenced Western thought since the seventeenth century, gets translated into *"ago, ergo sum"*: I am sure that I *am* precisely because I *do* something, whether that something be thinking or some other activity. So we tend to look upon our walking, talking, seeing, speaking, thinking, and other activities as if they constituted our personal identity. Apart from them we seem scarcely to exist.

Yet another problem we face in letting go is that we belong to a culture that is possessive and overanxious. Jesus said in the Sermon on the Mount: "Do not be anxious." He speaks about food and clothes and tells us that life is more important than food and the body more important than the clothes that cover it. This call of Jesus to surrender our anxieties can apply to our prayer. But we do not find it easy to let go of the things that cause fear, anxiety, and insecurity in our lives.

One of the great advantages of spending twenty to forty minutes each day in this prayer of "letting go" is that, while we may not be able to let go of our anxieties for good, we may be able to let go of them for these brief periods of time. To be able simply to be for twenty or forty minutes a day—without doing and without worrying—may help us to extend that sense of a new kind of identity (one we discover simply by being who we are in God) into some of the rest of our day. It may help us gradually to sight better perspectives and to set different priorities. We may come to learn that many of the things that once unsettled us we are now able to take in stride.

For inevitably this kind of contemplative exercise, faithfully adhered to, is going to give me a new sense of who I am. To be in the presence of God is to be in the presence of mystery: not only the mystery of God, but also the mystery of my own true self that is hidden in Him. My true identity, my uniqueness as a person can be found only in Him. Hence I can never be myself in separateness from God. What is of essential importance is what He does, not what I do; for He is the Source and Hidden Ground of who I am. Though I am distinct from God, I am not, and cannot be, separate from Him. This applies as well to my relationship with other persons. I am distinct from them: I am not who they are; yet I am not separate from them. For we all find our oneness, our identity, and our uniqueness in God. Because of this nonseparateness, what I do to my brother and sister I do to God and to myself. This sense of nondualism, nonseparateness, is the theological basis for nonviolence.

In contemplation we achieve what Merton speaks of in *The Wisdom of the Desert*, namely, we cross over "the abyss that separates us from ourselves" (p. 11). The statement is something like a Zen koan. For when we discover our true self, we haven't really crossed over anything (who would there be to do the crossing?). We simply *are* in God: one with Him, not separate from Him. What Merton is really saying is that, when I *am* myself, it is as if I have crossed an abyss — because what I was (or thought I was) is not really what I am. "Crossing the abyss" is simply becoming who I am and always have been. "On the other side" is my empirical ego that can never "cross over" because it exists only on the surface. When I discover myself and my true identity in God, I realize that there was no abyss and that the empirical ego actually has no substantive existence.

Contemplation is not a means to an end. It is not even a goal sought for itself. It is so utterly simple that the very desire for it becomes an obstacle to achieving it. And when you achieve it, you haven't really achieved anything. You do not get some place where you were not. You are getting where you always really are: in the presence of God. You have achieved nothing. Yet you have achieved everything. For you have been transformed in consciousness so that at last you recognize yourself for who you really are.

Perhaps someone will still persist: But what do I *do*, when I am doing nothing? Perhaps a simple summary might be suggested:

1. *Be quietly aware*, but without the need of an object to be aware of. You want to be aware of God, but not of God as a Being outside you;

2. *Be quiet* both within and without: no exterior words, no interior words;

3. *Be*, without thoughts, concepts, imaginings, desires, fears, concerns. Let there be nothing between you and God. When this happens, then you are in the darkness. All the lights by which ordinarily you know have been put out.

The Approach of
The Cloud of Unknowing

When the eyes of my mind have been darkened, then it may be that the eyes of my heart will be able to grasp God in love. So at least thought one of the great English mystics of the fourteenth century, the author of *The Cloud of Unknowing*. This anonymous work has achieved a good bit of popularity in recent years and a wide following. The fundamental thesis of the book — which I want to adopt wholeheartedly — is that, while we can think in praise and gratitude of God's wondrous works on our behalf (something surely we ought often to do), "no human person can think of God Himself" (Paulist Press edition, p. 133). Yet, he goes on to say that, though God cannot be thought, he certainly can be loved. "He can be taken and held by love but not by thought." In the exercise of contemplation, therefore, since one is seeking God Himself, one must put all things except God under a "cloud of forgetting." Once one does this, she/he is in darkness, for the normal lights by which we see have been put out. The darkness is a thick "cloud of unknowing," and one must be ready to strike at the cloud with the "sharp dart of longing love," seeking God Himself and nothing else. All that is needed is a simple reaching out to Him.

If the things you have banished under the "cloud of forgetting" seek to rise out of that cloud to intrude themselves on your consciousness, the author suggests the strategy of choosing a word, preferably one of a single syllable, like "God" or "love." "Fasten this word to your heart so that whatever happens it will never go away. The word is to be your shield and your spear" (p. 134). It will be your *shield*, for with it you will hold back whatever tries to emerge from beneath the "cloud of forgetting." It will be your *spear*, for with it you will beat upon the "cloud of unknowing" to pierce through, in love, to God.

In one sense the "cloud of unknowing" is darkness (since all our natural powers of knowing have been put out); yet it is, in another sense, the very luminosity of God. The reason it appears as darkness is because we are blinded by so much light. Thus the experience of contemplation might be compared to a plane that leaves the ground on a cloudy day. It rises higher and higher and enters into the clouds. At times the clouds are dark and at other times light and puffy, as if, in the latter cases, the sun was striving to break through. Then a moment is reached when one is on the other side of the clouds and sees the sun in all its blinding brilliance. The "cloud of unknowing" for those who have reached the other side becomes fused with the "cloud of forgetting." For the moment all is forgotten and we are wondrously and gloriously one with God.

The exercise of contemplation is a great need for the vast

majority of us who so often get caught up in the whirlwind of doing that there is grave danger we shall never allow ourselves the time just to be. Unless we find regular times simply to be, our doing will chop us up into bits; it will so compartmentalize our lives that we may never come to know who we *are*. Without contemplation we are in danger of losing, or never really discovering, our own identity. Unless we look, in love, to see the Face of the Invisible, we may ourselves turn out to be persons "without faces."

8

The Missing Rung: *Operatio*

We have completed our climb up Guigo's ladder or, more accurately, we have surveyed the four rungs of the ladder that according to him constitute the kind of exercise required of a person who is committed to a life of the spirit. It might be well at this point to make clear that you do not climb this ladder once and for all, as if, when you move from one rung to the next, you pull the previous one up with you. While Guigo makes it quite obvious that the highest rung of all and the one most to be cherished is contemplation, he nonetheless realizes that one does not easily achieve this rung; it does not flow from the other three with the same ease as they seem to flow from one another. He is clear also that one cannot stay on this highest rung for any great length of time. Hence one should not be loath to descend to the other rungs — indeed not only descend to them, but do so with the feeling that one is quite free to move about among them: now reading, now meditating, now praying.

When it comes to contemplation, however, we do not have the same freedom, that is to say, we are not always able to choose the moment when we shall ascend to this highest rung. To put it in the language we have used in the preceding chapter,

Portions of this chapter, which have appeared in modified form in an essay in *Toward an Integrated Humanity*, published by Cistercian Publications, are used with the publisher's permission.

we are not able to decide simply by an act of our will when we shall achieve that level of consciousness that is total awareness. Or to put it in a paraphrase of Guigo's words: Our inner spirit is too weak to bear the brilliance of the divine light for very long. So, once it has experienced that light, let our inner spirit descend, gently and gradually, to one or other of the three steps by which it made its ascent to contemplation. Let it rest now in one, now in another. It is with some regret that Guigo finds himself saying this, convinced as he is that a person is nearer to God the higher he/she is able to climb beyond the first rung of the ladder. But such, he remarks sadly, is the frailty and wretchedness of the human condition that it is but rarely and briefly that we are able to enjoy the fullness of contemplative joy.

It may well be that the adverb "sadly" is too strong a term to describe Guigo's sentiments as they emerge from his "Letter." It might have been better to say: "He remarks with a spirit of resignation," or perhaps even "with a note of realism." For, after all, even though he defers to Brother Gervase as the one who has truly experienced the kind of spiritual exercise of which he is speaking, we can presume that Guigo was not without his own experience of the various rungs of that spiritual ladder, including the topmost one. From that experience he would have come to an understanding of the limitations human nature imposes on us (whether we use the term "frailty" or "wretchedness" to describe them or prefer a less pejorative term) and to an acceptance of them. In fact, in a switch of metaphors, Guigo makes quite clear that the sweetness of contemplation is something that one should not normally expect to be prolonged. Moving from the contemplative ladder to the mystical mountain, he identifies the contemplative experience with what happened to Peter and John (he ignores James!) on the mountain of the transfiguration. He not only switches metaphors, he doubles them. For he also describes the transfiguration experience in terms of the bridal image. Guigo has Peter and John lingering for a while on the mountaintop, enjoying the glory of the Spouse. But the Spouse, so long awaited, soon withdraws and is gone. Yet—and this is the consolation tempering the sadness of which Guigo speaks—the Spouse is not really gone. For even when the sweetness of contemplation has come to an end, He yet stays with us to direct us, to fill us with His grace, and to unite us ever more fully with Himself.

What Guigo is saying here, it seems to me, is that even when the vivid experience of God's presence—which may come to us in the "exercise" of contemplation—disappears, the contemplative dimension of our lives continues to be a reality. Though we may not have total awareness of it, we are nonetheless always in God as the Source and Ground of love in whom we find our identity and uniqueness. For, as we have discussed earlier, we are contemplatives at the very core of our being. Nothing can change that. But our perception and awareness of it varies a great deal from deep experience of it to a semiconscious awareness that remains habitually as a kind of backdrop for our lives—especially if we are serious about times of silence and solitude each day.

One might want to go farther than Guigo and suggest that coming down from the mountaintop or from the topmost rung of the ladder is not just a regrettable necessity, it is an imperative of the Christian vocation. Part of that "imperative" is the tradition of *contemplata tradere*—the obligation we have to share with others the insights that contemplation brings. For a Christian, living on this side of the eschatological divide, there is much work to be done. The Good News of faith needs to be proclaimed. The reign of God remains yet to be fully established. Structures that exist in our world that enslave and impoverish people need to be redeemed so that they enhance human dignity rather than destroy it.

The four rungs of Guigo's ladder imply a *fuga mundi* that might be acceptable in a monastic community (though today many monks are reexamining the meaning of "flight from the world," and Thomas Merton's writings have exercised an enormous influence in that reexamination). But Christians today (monks or nonmonks) cannot ignore the call of Vatican II to deeper involvement in building a better world. Thus we read in *Gaudium et Spes*:

> . . . Men are not deterred by the Christian message from building up the world, or impelled to neglect the welfare of their fellows. They are, rather, more stringently bound to do these things. (no. 34)

Again:

> Earthly progress must be carefully distinguished from the growth of Christ's kingdom. Nevertheless, to the extent that the former can contribute to the better ordering of human society, it is of vital concern to the kingdom of God. For after we have obeyed the Lord, and in His Spirit nurtured on earth the values of human dignity, brotherhood and freedom, and indeed all the good fruits of our nature and enterprise, we will find them again, but freed of stain, burnished and transfigured. (no. 39)

The Missing Rung

In the light of our common responsibility to promote in our world the dignity and the rights of human persons, I would venture to suggest that Guigo's ladder needs another rung. The "missing rung" in Guigo's ladder is *operatio* or action. By "action" I intend to signify especially (though not exclusively) social action: engagement or involvement in the kind of action that will contribute to the bettering of the social conditions that affect peoples' lives.

Before discussing the nature of this social action, I want to remind the reader that Guigo in his *Ladder of Monks* is using a literary device. He says that the notion of the four rungs of the ladder came to him while he was at work in the fields. This can hardly be taken as literally true. He certainly knew of these steps from a long and living tradition that had been handed on to him from the Christian past. In fact, to be quite explicit, a similar "ladder" was "constructed" some fifty years earlier by a writer whose works Guigo could be expected to have known, Hugh of St. Victor.

Hugh of St. Victor

In the seven books he wrote on the liberal arts (*Eruditionis Didascalicae*), Hugh writes, in book five, about the five steps that constitute the "exercise" of a person bent on leading a spiritual life. Like Guigo, he assigns a place that is unique and the highest of all to contemplation. But he speaks, significantly, of four, rather than three, steps that precede it. The four steps are *lectio*, *meditatio*, *oratio*, and *operatio*. By reading one achieves understanding, and through meditation one sees a plan of action beginning to form. Hugh speaks of *consilium* (which I translate, somewhat freely, as "seeing a plan of action beginning to form") coming from meditation. Our plans, however, will be "weak and inefficacious" without help from God. This help we seek in prayer (*oratio*). God enlightens us by His grace before we act; He also accompanies us with His grace as we act, directing our steps in the way of peace. Thus it is He who works alongside us in reaching the fourth step, namely, "effecting the good work" (*operatio*) that needs to be accomplished.

One can only guess as to why Guigo omitted *operatio* from his "ladder." Perhaps he felt the additional rung was not necessary for monks, though it would be for the rest of us. I need not point out — at least to those who are familiar with his writings in the 1960s — that Thomas Merton would have had strong reservations about such a position. At any rate, since this book is not primarily directed to monks, it will be appropriate, and indeed necessary, for us to consider "the missing rung" in Guigo's ladder.

The Christian Choice and Task for the World

One whose prayer and meditation leads him/her to look at the society in which he/she lives will come to understand that we all face a choice and a task. The *choice* is either a society of persons conscious of community and communion, or a society of isolated individuals drowned in the nameless separateness and the unredeemed alienation of the collectivity. What complicates our *choice* is the power in our society of an ever more sophisticated technology that in theory can serve either the community or the collectivity, but in fact seems to be moving us almost relentlessly away from the community and toward the shallow emptiness of the collectivity.

If this is the choice we face, the *task* that we are called to is the struggle to build the human community—with its values of human dignity, human freedom and with its opportunities for solitude and contemplation. Failure to engage in this *task* (the *operatio*, so it seems to me, for our age) can mean but one thing: being absorbed almost helplessly into the collectivity, in which men and women give up their freedom of thought and action and become part of the system that controls them and all of human life.

The community is the place of freedom. It is the home of the person, who is linked with his/her brothers and sisters in the unity of all that makes them human and in a sharing of all that makes them one in Christ. In the community there is an awareness that, though each of us is unique and distinct as persons, we are nonetheless not separate. For we are all one in that Hidden Ground of Love whom we experience in contemplation and in whom we find our identity and our uniqueness. Christ, in whom as Paul says the fullness of the godhead resides by God's design, is the archetype of the person living in community. To be a person is for the Christian "to be in Christ." It is in the context of community that persons experience the call to and the opportunity for solitude and contemplation.

The collectivity, on the other hand, is the place of slavery.

The individual is simply a unit in the collectivity divided off from all other units. He/she is a single separate being, definable only in negative terms: he/she is not "someone else." "Individuals" who comprise the collectivity, live in isolation and alienation from one another. They are "united" only superficially by an external uniformity that has scarcely any relationship with the inner realities of the human spirit. This "mass society" is the place, not of contemplation, but of what Pascal calls "*divertissement*," an untranslatable word that roughly means "distraction" or "diversion"; it is the escape from life's problems and invitations into activities that in ultimate terms are meaningless. People whose lives are shaped by the collectivity are people who have lost their sense of the transcendent. This means that they are deprived of their natural capacity for contemplation.

The Sickness of Mass Society
In an essay that has become something of a classic ("Rain and the Rhinoceros" in *Raids on the Unspeakable*) Merton diagnoses the sickness of this mass society, which has forfeited its sense of solitude and its capacity for contemplation, as "rhinoceritis." He draws on Eugene Ionesco's powerful play *Rhinoceros* to illustrate the hapless state of the collectivity. In this play everyone except Beranger becomes a victim of "rhinoceritis." This disease consists in compliance with whatever is the norm of the moment, no matter how absurd it may be. Everyone becomes a rhinoceros. Beranger is the last human being left on earth, the last person. He feels a strong urge to abandon his humanness and join the herd, but something deep in him prevents him from doing so. He persists in remaining human in what has become a nonhuman world.

Ionesco, in his own *Notes* on his writings, makes the point that it is only solitude, which is proper to the community, that can save people from the slavery of unthinking conformity that is the characteristic of the collectivity. Thus he writes:

Forms of rhinoceritis of every kind, from left and right, are there to threaten mankind when men have no time to think or collect themselves; and they lie in wait for mankind today, because we have lost all feeling and taste for genuine solitude. For solitude is not *separation* but *mediation*. (*Notes and Counternotes: Writings on the Theatre*, trans. Donald Watson [New York: Grove Press, 1964], p. 151)

It would, of course, be a misunderstanding to think that either the community or the collectivity exists in a pure state. There is a bit of each in all of us. Our task is to expose — in ourselves as well as in our society — the illusions that the collectivity lives by and to work for the building up of the community. What is especially significant for our day is that the ongoing dialectic between the community and the collectivity takes place within the context of an everescalating technology. I want to stress the fact of the rapid escalation of technology in our time. For it has certainly been true since the time of the Industrial Revolution, and probably to some extent through the whole of human history, that technology has had a strong voice in determining whether it will be the values of the community or the collectivity that will predominate in a particular society. I would venture to say that there has never been an age where its voice has been so strong and its influence so widespread and all-pervasive as in ours.

Technology
Technology, considered in itself and apart from the circumstances in which it operates, is neither good nor bad. Yet in the concrete it is never neutral: it either builds or destroys the commonweal; it either serves or exploits the human family. And it would appear that quite consistently throughout history technology tends to move in the direction of destructiveness and exploitation rather than toward building and service. At least this is true when society has not been guided by wisdom;

and it seems correct to say that the grim reality of history is that technology has seldom been in the hands of the truly wise.

The reason that technology can easily become anticommunity is that its general thrust is away from such things as human dignity and equality, neighborly love and compassion (the things that make for community) and toward those things that foster the mood of the collectivity. I presume there would be those who would want to dispute such a thesis. I am prepared to defend it, however, because it seems to me that the intrinsic goals of technology (namely, what it seems to tend toward of itself, apart from the personal motivation that may direct particular technologists) are power and profit, with the means to those intrinsic goals being greater and greater efficiency. Great power and enormous profit, because they do not seem easily capable of being shared, tend to separate rather than unite people. Power almost of necessity tends to be concentrated in the hands of the few at the expense of the many; and profit-oriented endeavors tend to enrich the already wealthy and to increase the poverty of the already poor.

This is not to say that technology has not achieved many benefits that have improved the style of human living and made life more comfortable. But it is necessary to ask whether these undeniable material advantages have not been gained at the price of true spiritual goods. We have built fantastic ways of transportation that make it possible for people to go anywhere they want; yet the irony is that we live in an age that has lost its sense of direction. Physically we can go wherever we want to, even to the moon and probably to Mars, but spiritually many among us have no notion of where we really want to go.

There are the everincreasing marvels of modern communication. No more than a few generations ago a person could not be heard beyond the range of his/her own voice. Now we have the technological capability of communicating with the entire globe. Yet we have to face the uneasy question: "Given the fact that we can speak to the whole world, do we have anything that is worth saying? Do we have the wisdom to say the things that will be for the peace and betterment of the world?" Henry David Thoreau (1817–1862) — a person who took a rather dim view of technological advances — was told one day that inventors were on the verge of producing a technology that would eventually make it possible for people in New York City to speak with people in New Orleans. His sensible question was: "What if they don't have anything to say?"

His question remains valid today. The miracle of modern communication systems has brought people together so that their destinies are intertwined. But have we yet learned to speak to one another? We have suddenly come to realize that the word "communication" can mean two quite different things. It can mean being able physically to be in touch with others; or it can mean being able to reach their hearts, so that communication leads to communion. There is little point in being able to get in touch with people all over the world unless we can reach their inner spirits. And this we can do only if we believe that all men and women are brothers and sisters who are united to one another spiritually and ecologically in a fellowship that is global in its dimensions. It must be our common task to build that fellowship for the good of the whole human race. This calls for wisdom: the wisdom that alone can build community and expose the illusions of the collectivity.

I should perhaps confess to the unwary reader that in much of what I am saying about technology I am being influenced by Merton, though I do not want to make him responsible for anything I say other than what I quote from him directly. It would be wrong to say that Merton was oblivious of the wondrous advances technology has made. For instance, in early 1968 he welcomed the addition, including indoor plumbing, that was built onto his hermitage. He counted it a distinct advantage that he no longer had to face regular encounters with the "bastard," as he had "affectionately" named the snake who had staked equal claims to the outhouse that had served Merton's needs in his first years in the hermitage. It would be equally true to say that Merton enjoyed his typewriter for writing and his refrigerator for keeping his beer cool.

Merton never wrote a book on technology, though he read widely on the topic (he admired what Jacques Ellul and Lewis Mumford had to say on this issue); there are, however, significant references in *Conjectures of a Guilty Bystander*, a collection made from entries kept in journals over a period of years and published in 1966. In a circular letter sent to many of his friends in mimeographed form in Lent of 1967 Merton attempts to answer the question that some people asked after reading *Conjectures*: "Am I against technology?" He writes:

> Obviously I am not maintaining that we ought to get rid of matches and go back to making fires by rubbing sticks together . . . Nor am I maintaining that modern transportation, medicine, methods of production and so on are "bad." I am glad to have a gas heater this winter since I can't cut wood. Yet I am not saying that I am a better human being this winter when I have more "leisure," than I was last winter when I did a lot of chopping. Nothing wrong with chopping either. What I question is the universal myth that technology infallibly makes everything in every way better for everybody. It does not.

He goes on to discuss how technological advance can be used to help people or to destroy them.

> Thank God for the fact that penicillin saves thousands of lives. But let's face the fact that penicillin saves lives for people whom society then allows to starve because it is not set up to feed them. If it used its technological resources well, society could certainly feed them. In fact it doesn't.

He speaks too of what technology has done in the underdeveloped countries of the world. Multinational corporations have gone into financially backward nations with a setup that works fine in affluent countries, but can be disastrous in countries that are poor. What happens is that these corporations bring huge profits back to their own country and often dislocate the people of the "backward country" — many of whom move to the city seeking work only to find themselves living in even more abject poverty. Why? Because technology, by developing labor-saving methods of production, has reduced instead of increased the number of jobs available to them. This is technology in the service not of people but of profit.

One of the chief faults of technology is that it is so often afflicted with a false ethic that gives priority to material progress over moral growth and to efficiency in getting things done over social responsibility. A technology whose overriding imperative is what can be done must be done, is ill-prepared to heed the wisdom which could present basic human values that might offer compelling reasons for not doing something that we have the power to do. This drive to make the possible real can threaten the values of the community even as it helps to construct the illusions of the collectivity.

Perhaps a subtler form of technology's failure in its choice of goals is the lack of a proper balance or sense of hierarchy in that choice, even when worthwhile goals are chosen. Granted that we cannot do everything, because time, energy, and funds are limited, priority decisions must be made among the possible goods that can be worked for. Too often basic human needs are ignored for the sake of scientific accomplishments. Too often the exotic is preferred to the ordinary. It is all very exciting (though with repetition the excitement quickly begins to wear off) to put satellites in space or even dramatically to repair those that have broken down there. There is a sense of acting like God when He made the stars and put them in the heavens. Yet is peopling the heavens our most pressing task? Do we not have a greater responsibility to feed those who people the earth?

In 1961 President John F. Kennedy promised that by the end of the decade the United States would put a man on the moon.

On July 20, 1969, it happened: Neil Armstrong stepped out of his Apollo spaceship onto the moon. A marvelous accomplishment indeed. It was science fiction come true. But suppose that President Kennedy in 1961 had said: By the end of this decade we shall eliminate starvation from the face of the Earth? Could we have done it? The answer of course we do not know. But should we have tried? Did the choice to put people on the moon prevent us from making the choice to put food in the mouths of all the men, women, and children on our own planet? We have to face the question: In our technological choices does the service of people often yield place to scientific discovery?

We have discussed some of the things that technology can fail to do. It is also worth asking the question: What has it done for people? And there is no doubt that we can point to many wonderful accomplishments that have eased work and given people more time for leisure. Still we have to look at the fact that for vast numbers of people technology has dulled the creativity of the human spirit. It has made work boring, routine, and monotonous — so much so that the worker's sense of his own worth and pride in his own creative powers have been diminished by the very work that ought to increase them. The consequence is that work becomes something to be escaped from as quickly and as often as possible. Workers are thus drawn into the vortex of *divertissement*, or "distraction," in which they strive to lose themselves in activities that are mindless and without any real human significance. The soap opera of television has become the stereotype of this sort of soporific activity. Such *divertissment* moves people in the direction of the collectivity rather than the community.

Technology can also project an aura of omnipotence. It can be a modern secular type of the fifth-century heresy of Pelagianism. The Pelagians said that we could save ourselves. Our own efforts were all that we needed; we did not need the grace of God. So the myth of an omnipotent technology says: We can run our own universe; we have the technological skill. Our machinery is sufficient for all our needs and there is nothing that science cannot do for us.

Technology and "The Angels"

In 1967 Thomas Merton published an article on angels in a small magazine called *Season*. The article is both whimsical and at the same time in deadly earnest. Entitled "The Angel and the Machine," it shows how the angels, once thought to be our helpers in carrying out God's plans, have been replaced by the machine. He writes:

> Technological civilization is . . . a civilization without angels . . . in which we have chosen the machine instead of the angel: that is to say we have placed the machine where the angels used to be: at the limits of our own strength, at the frontier of our natural capacity.

We need the angels, he suggests, not to replace our machines, but to teach us how to live with them.

> For the angels come to us to teach us how to rest, to forget useless care, to relax, in silence, to "let go," to abandon ourselves not in self-conscious fun but in self-forgetful faith. We need the angels to remind us that we can get along without so many superfluous goods and satisfactions which instead of lightening our existence weigh it down. May they come back into our world and deliver it from its massive boredom, its metaphysical fatigue.

What he is saying is that we must and we can live in the world of the machine, the world of technology, and still build the community. But we need the wisdom that comes from God: a wisdom that earlier ages personified in the form of superhuman beings. Without needing to explain what precisely earlier ages meant by these angelic beings, we need the wisdom they personified, the wisdom that was their message from God.

Almost all societies have recognized the "way of wisdom." It has been respected not as a flight into illusion, but as a return to reality in its hidden ground and roots. Indeed special homage has been paid to those people who have attained to the inner meaning of life and being, who have articulated this meaning for their brothers and sisters, and who have been able to unite in themselves the divisions and complications that tend to confuse the lives of their fellow-men and women. This can also happen in a technological society, but only if it is ready to renounce its obsession with the triumph of the isolated individual and the collective will to power — in order to adopt a different view of reality: one that springs from solitude and contemplation and constitutes the life of the community.

The intent of this chapter has been to discuss the "missing rung" of Guigo's "ladder" of spiritual exercise. Following Hugh of St. Victor, I have suggested that the "missing rung" is *operatio* — though I have given it a meaning that may or may not be what Hugh had in mind. I have suggested that *operatio* today means "social engagement" and that social engagement means building community. I have tried to show, ever so briefly, what that building entails in a society irrevocably committed to a very sophisticated technology that touches people's lives with ever-increasing intimacy. I have not intended to picture technology as the enemy of the community, though I have tried to point out the special problems it poses and the unconscious plea that it would seem to be making for a wisdom that alone can set human life moving in the right direction.

In an earlier chapter I quoted the moving words of Psalm 116: "I will walk in the presence of the Lord in the land of the living." This is a fruitful text for reflection on the content of this chapter. "The land of the living," I would like to suggest, may be taken to mean the concrete situation of our own time and culture in which we strive to build the community, that is to say, in which we try to carry out the *operatio* to which "reading" and "meditation" have called us. I have attempted in this chapter to highlight the all-pervasive influence of technology in the culture and civilization of our time. It is of course not the only influence we have to deal with in our efforts to work for community, but it enters into so many aspects of our lives that it would be folly to ignore it. In our time it is very much a part of "the land of the living."

"Walking in the presence of the Lord," the mind-set and the heart-set that emerge from contemplation, furnishes the background out of which alone it becomes possible for us to do this "work" to which we are called. Or to put this in another way: Whereas "reading" and "meditation" call us to the "*operatio*" of building community in a world of multiplicity, "contemplation" offers us a new and different understanding of that same world. This understanding goes beyond the surface dualism that we tend to perceive. Because it is the experience of the unity of all things and especially of all persons in God (in whom all find their identity and uniqueness), it offers a vision of community: not just a vision of what it should become, but a vision of what at the deepest level of reality it actually is. Contemplation enables us to see that community is God's primordial gift. It is, therefore, not so much something that needs to be created as something that needs to be realized. There is a level of perception where we are able to see that we do not really build community: we accept it. This of course is not to say that the acceptance happens without struggle. It is just that the contemplative perspective can enlighten us on the true nature of the struggle and the goal it must seek. We do not produce what is already there; we do have to discover it.

9

Guigo's Ladder
and Gandhi's *Satyagraha*

In chapter 5, when discussing the meaning of the biblical term
metanoia, or "conversion," I spoke of what I considered as three
significant "conversion moments" in my own life. The third was
a conversion that more and more Christians have experienced
in our day, namely, the conversion to nonviolence. The curious
fact about this conversion is that many who have experienced it
have been brought to it, initially at least, through their contact
with non-Christian sources. For much of what contemporary
Christians have to say about nonviolence has come, I think it is
fair to say, from a man who was not a Christian, namely,
Mohandas Gandhi, though—and there is surely an irony in
this—Gandhi first learned about nonviolence from Christian
sources. It was his reading of the New Testament and his discovery of the nonviolence of Jesus that sent him back to his own
Indian scriptures. Nonviolence had been present there, but
strange to say, he had not seen it there till he had reflected
deeply on the Sermon on the Mount. It is surely a sign of the
unity of so many deep religious perceptions that it was Jesus
who taught Gandhi how to read the *Bhagavad Gita*! For a goodly
number of Christians the journey has been in the opposite
direction: they found nonviolence in Gandhi before they were
able to find it in their own Christian Scriptures. Gandhi taught
them how to read the Sermon on the Mount!

I introduce Gandhi into this book on prayer and Christian spirituality because I hope to show, in the present chapter, that nonviolence and contemplation are closely linked. A contemplative, because of the perception of reality that contemplation gives him/her, must — this at least is my belief — be committed in one way or another to nonviolence; moreover, I do not think that a person can be truly nonviolent without the vision that only contemplation is able to bring.

Much of this book has centered on Guigo's ladder of spiritual exercise that leads a person to the perfection of contemplation. Though he did not speak of it in such terms, I think perhaps we might talk about Gandhi's ladder that one must climb to reach the perfection of nonviolence. Such a ladder would have three rungs.

Ahimsa as the First Rung of the Gandhian Ladder

The first "rung" on Gandhi's ladder is *ahimsa*, a Sanskrit word that means "noninjury." It is the efficacious concern to do no harm, physical or psychological, to another person. Though at first hearing *ahimsa* may seem to express an attitude that is negative, in actual fact it designates, as Gandhi perceived it, something very positive: namely, that I have a concern, a love, a spirit of good will toward another that makes it impossible for me to inflict injury on that person. The motivation of *ahimsa* is nothing less than unconditional love for people. This unconditional love flows from the conviction that essentially we are one and therefore we can — all of us — respond to the overtures of love.

Ahimsa and Contemplation

It ought to be clear, then, that the fundamental motivation that inspires *ahimsa* is an intuition that comes from contemplation, namely, the belief in, and to some degree the actual experience of, our oneness with one another in God. Moreover, it may be said that if contemplation frees us from the tyranny of a false activism that tends to separate what we do from what we are, *ahimsa* helps us to unite action and being. For it is action that flows from the reality of being grounded in love and, therefore, wanting to let love — which always tends toward unity — transform our relationships with people. *Ahimsa*, therefore, tends to unite what I do with who I am. For it removes from me the destructive forces that not only divide me from my brothers and sisters, but also from my own true reality, my own true self, and make me a prisoner of my own illusions.

Yet if I am to remove the destructive force of violence from my relationship with others, I must put something else in its place; otherwise *ahimsa* would simply mean a vacuum of passivity and open vulnerability. The positive force that I must substitute for the destructive force of violence is what Gandhi called *satyagraha*, which we may see as the second "rung" of the Gandhian ladder.

Satyagraha as the Second Rung

In his initial efforts to practice what I am calling "nonviolence," Gandhi used the phrase "passive resistance." In 1906, in the early phase of his South African struggle to achieve elemental human rights for Indian immigrants, he invited his followers to suggest a more appropriate name to designate this struggle for equality that they were engaged in. One suggestion, offered by his nephew, Manganlal Gandhi, was *sadagraha*, which means "firmness in a good cause." Gandhi accepted this suggestion, but with some modification. He substituted for *sada* the Sanskrit word for truth, *satya*. Thus the name that became the designation for the Gandhian approach to dealing with conflicts became *satyagraha*, which means, literally, "firmness in the truth" or even the "persistence of truth." Gandhi defined it as

"the force which is born of truth and love." For Gandhi truth
and love are always closely related. Thus he says: "The sword of
satyagraha is love, and the unshakable firmness that comes from
it." *Satyagraha* may be described as a moral quality in persons
whereby they are firmly committed to the truth. It may also be
thought of as a metaphysical reality: Truth as "that which is"
and therefore that which ultimately cannot be negated or frus-
trated. It will, finally, prevail. One might say that *satyagraha*
means at one and the same time: "We shall overcome, if we are
dynamically committed to the truth," and "Truth shall overcome, because it is the ultimate Reality." It is the second statement that makes the first possible. It is precisely insofar as we
are committed to the ultimate Reality and united with it that
we can overcome violence, oppression, and conflict.

This term adopted by Gandhi may well have undercurrents
flowing out of the Sermon on the Mount, which concludes with
Jesus' words likening one who hears his words and puts them
into practice to a person who builds his house firmly on rock
instead of on shifting sands that offer no stability. It may also be
noted that the second Epistle of Peter is addressed to followers
of Jesus who are "firmly rooted in the truth" (1:12). *Satyagraha*,
then, understood as a *means* (as distinguished from the meaning
it has as an *end*, namely, the ultimate Truth) is a moral force,
firmly rooted in truth and love, that puts itself at the service of
justice and peace. *Satyagraha*, which opposes evil with serious
and positive, though nonviolent, resistance in order to overcome it with good, must be distinguished from what Gandhi
called "the nonviolence of the weak," which simply submits to
evil without resistance. It was a fundamental principle of Gandhi's way of life that *evil must always be resisted*, but in ways and by
methods of action that are nonviolent. To answer violence with
violence is to surrender to the aggressor; for it means letting
him/her choose the "weapons" for resolving conflict and dis-
agreement. More than that it means that there is more violence

in the world and, therefore, more likelihood of moving farther from, rather than closer to, justice and peace.

I must not resist an aggressor with violence; yet I must remain in control of the situation not by the power of force, but through truth and love. I must always *express* the truth and confront the adversary with the truth. At the same time I must always *look for* the truth that is in the other. It may be there but hidden. Part of my task as a nonviolent person is to try to discover it. I must always *express* love, but also I must always *look for* love. And I must understand that it may be expressed in such a clumsy way that it is obscured and easy for me to miss. Nonviolence has a keen eye for the *truth* and the *love* that are in the other, but so hidden that only the most sensitive heart can perceive them.

Satyagraha and Contemplation

This "keen eye" is a gift born of contemplation. For this desire to find the truth and goodness in the other person is part of the contemplative vision. The contemplative believes, and in some obscure way knows, that each person finds his identity and uniqueness in God and therefore in essential Goodness. This imaging of God's goodness in the other may be shrouded by a mask of falseness and illusion, but a true contemplative can never deny that it is present, even in those situations where it may seem remote and impossible to reach.

Ahimsa and *Satyagraha* are ways to overcome violence. Yet they may not achieve that result — at least not immediately. This must not deter us from taking these stances. I do not tell the truth simply in order to get results, but first and foremost because the truth must be expressed. I do not love in order to receive a return of love, but because love is what I must do. I speak the truth and act out of love with the hope that thereby good results may come; but while that hope of results *accompanies* what I do, it cannot be the principal motive of my action.

The Third Rung: *Nishkama-karma*

This leads to what I would call the third "rung" of the Gandhian ladder: *nishkama-karma*. Because he was a Hindu, the reality of *karma* and the law of *karma* would have strongly influenced Gandhi's thinking. The law of *karma* concerns the inevitable and inexorable effect that our every action has on us. There is no escape from the welcome or the unwelcome consequences of our minutest thoughts and actions. The only salvation from this inevitable link of consequences to actions is to perform one's actions in such a way that one lets go of attachment to the consequences of his/her actions. This is the meaning of *nishkama-karma*. Literally it means action without desire. *Nishkama-karma* detaches us, as it were, from the chain of action-reaction. "In *nishkama-karma* action having been started unilaterally and with no thought of its consequences, the fangs, as it were, of the law of action and reaction to touch or hurt us are removed. The nonattached [person], who performs actions only because he considers it his duty and not because he has bargained for results, has liberated himself from the chain of action and consequences" (S. K. Saksena, in Charles A. Moore, *The Indian Mind* [University of Hawaii Press, 1967], pp. 34–35). *Nishkama-karma* simply means that one does his/her duty (*dharma*). Whether doing it will achieve the result of peace or conflict resolution, I cannot tell; and while I am not uninterested in the outcome, my principal motivation must be not to achieve some desired result but to embody truth and love in what I do.

Whether one accepts the law of *karma* or not doesn't really matter. For once the actions, which I perform and into which I try to put truth and love, get into the public forum they mingle with the actions of others (over which I may have little or no control) and their direction may be changed. They may not be able to achieve the end I might have hoped for when I performed them. Though they seem to fail, I must still do the truth and the loving thing. This is the meaning of *nishkama-karma*: I do what I must do regardless of the results.

Nishkama-karma and Contemplation

It should be clear that *nishkama-karma* as a way to nonviolence has an obvious kinship with that "letting go" which is the necessary precondition of contemplation. Contemplation requires that I let go of all that is not God so that I may experience the presence of God. *Nishkama-karma* requires that I let go of the fruits of what I do so that my acts may truly be in the service of truth and love.

Ahimsa, satyagraha, and *nishkama-karma* — these three, I have suggested, form the three rungs of the Gandhian ladder of nonviolence. Yet I probably ought to admit that to describe these as rungs of a ladder could be a misleading analogy, and for this reason perhaps it ought to be abandoned. For while the rungs of Guigo's ladder are *interrelated* in such a way that one leads to the other (we noted how for the first three at least Guigo says a person is "sent" from one to the other and is quite free to move from one to the other), the "rungs" of Gandhi's "ladder" are so *interdependent* that one cannot be conceived as existing without the other. It is as if — supposing the analogy be retained at least for the moment — his "ladder" is carved out of a single piece of wood. Or, to abandon the ladder analogy altogether, Gandhi's threefold approach to the meaning of nonviolence has very much in common with Guigo's understanding of contemplation. In both cases, we are speaking not primarily of an exercise or a program of action that someone performs, but more deeply about a way of life, a "dimension" of human living that offers new directions to the way in which people live out their lives.

The Unity of Contemplation and Nonviolence

Contemplation is an experienced awareness of God in which one comes to realize the unity of all reality. Nonviolence is the living out of that unity in such a way that it motivates us to treat all people — whether "the just or the unjust" — with respect and pushes us to look for the truth and goodness in them that transcend all creaturely limitation. This is but a way of saying that the nonviolent person seeks to find in all people what the contemplative already sees (though in the obscurity of faith), namely, that Hidden Ground of Love, in which all things find their being, their identity, and their uniqueness and which the Christian contemplative calls God. Contemplation and nonviolence are so intimately related in their fundamental intuitions that I find it difficult—as I have already said—to see how one can be truly contemplative without at the same time being nonviolent. Equally, I cannot see how a person can choose nonviolence as a way of life if he/she does not, in some way or other, possess the contemplative vision.

Nonviolence and the Christian Story

At this point someone might want to pose the question: Where were Christian thinkers all these centuries, if it had to be left to a twentieth-century Hindu to discover the nonviolence of Jesus? Such a question might produce a variety of answers. I can think of at least three. (1) One answer could be: Some Christians, notably the "peace churches" (such as the Quakers, the Mennonites, the Brethren), as well as some groups in other churches, did discover and proclaim the nonviolence of Jesus. (2) From other quarters might come the answer: What Gandhi found in the New Testament isn't really there; nonviolence was not a part of the teaching of Jesus. (3) Yet another response might be that some Christians were so occupied with "baptizing" the "just-war theory" that they thought they had found it in the New Testament and, therefore, there was no need for further scriptural inquiry into the morality of war. The first answer is surely correct. The second answer is debatable, and I would want to come out on the other side of the debate and maintain the nonviolence of Jesus. The third statement is probably a reasonably accurate summary of the history of the attitude toward war and violence in the history of the Christian Church (at least the Roman Catholic Church) since the days of the Emperor Constantine.

I may perhaps speak of myself as a fairly representative example, for all too many years of my life, of a post-Constantinian–just-war-theory Roman Catholic. When I first began any serious and formal study of moral issues, I was in a seminary. The time was the period of World War II. One would expect that as seminarians studying moral theology we would have been deeply concerned about the war and the morality of the way in which it was being conducted. Yet, strangely, I do not remember any discussion of such matters in class or among my fellow seminarians. Almost certainly we would have discussed the issue of war in our study of the fifth Commandment: "Thou shalt not kill," in which we would have talked about the right of self-defense against an unjust aggressor: a right that would have been extended to nations as well as individuals. I am certain, too, that we would have discussed the principles of the "just-war theory." For a long time in my life I accepted them as fundamental Christian principles, even though I knew that they had come, not from the Gospel, but from Greek and Roman ethical thought. It was enough for me that they had been "baptized" by St. Augustine and confirmed by St. Thomas Aquinas. They were — so it seemed to me — very much a part of our Roman Catholic baggage. Yet I do not recall any effort on my own or on the part of those who taught me to apply them to the war that was being fought at the time. I apparently took it for granted that, if we were involved in a war, it would be a just war and that justice (and therefore God also) would be on our side. As Merton once said: "God is always the first One to be enlisted in war."

World War II came to an end and I recall joining in the jubilation that Hitler had been defeated and the Pearl Harbor disaster turned about. I do remember having some qualms — I cannot really recall how deeply — about the saturation-and-fire-bombing of German cities and especially about the dropping of two atomic bombs on Japanese cities in 1945. But apparently these concerns did not cause me any sleepless nights or move me to speak out on such issues.

But I also remember a gradual changing of my attitude toward war in the mid-sixties when we had become deeply imbedded in the struggle in Viet Nam. For the first time ever, I began to question the justice of our involvement in a particular war. In fact, just recently, in an attempt to recapture my feelings about war in the mid-sixties. I unearthed a box of long-forgotten sermons and discovered one I had given to college students on February 19, 1967. In it I spoke of a pastoral letter — on the immorality of abortion — that the American bishops had issued the previous week. I suggested that we must not let our sense of the sacredness of human life decay and, further, that we needed to think of this commitment to life not only with regard to abortion, but also in terms of the kind of national commitment we had made in Viet Nam. I said: "We have to ask searching questions about the war. Are we equating our Christianity with patriotism? Must we not ask and demand that our government ask whether the extent of our commitment does not outweigh the good we hope to achieve?" I shall quote no more, as I do not want to bore the reader with a twenty-year-old sermon. Yet I need to say that I could not help but notice, as I looked over that ancient bit of pulpiteering, that all the arguments I gave for my position were based on reason. I said not a single thing about the Gospel or about the example of Jesus. But then why should I have been expected to? It was an application of the principles of the "just-war theory" that was called for in this situation. After all, that is what I had been taught.

From the "Just-War" Doctrine to the Gospel

Though I made it clear in my Preface that I do not want this book to be unduly autobiographical, I do feel at this point the need to add that at the time of my life that I am speaking about something else was happening in my life — something that I also referred to in chapter 5 as yet another "conversion" that I experienced. I discovered the Bible and a whole new way of experiencing what it meant to read it. I came to see that it was a misuse of the Scriptures to build a moral case out of arguments from reason and then go to Scripture for texts to bolster these arguments. Rather we must turn to the Scriptures to see what is God's call to us. What are the directions in which He wishes us to move? What are the qualities that must mark us as His followers?

It is not difficult to see what this means about the approach we must take toward war and especially toward nuclear war. We must go to the Bible not in search of reasons that will support the "theory of the just war," but to see what God wants of us. If we are truly committed Christians, we will approach the Bible not to ask the question: Is war justified? but rather to ask: What is the responsibility of a disciple of Jesus with regard to the waging of war and the making of peace?

One does not have to read very far into the Scriptures to come to the realization that a follower of Jesus is intended to be a peacemaker, a reconciler whose task is to help to put back together a broken humanity. The one beatitude that has as its reward the entitlement of being God's children is the beatitude of the peacemakers: "Blessed are the peacemakers, they shall be called the children of God" (Matt. 5:9).

The word that is used for peace in the New Testament, *eirene*, is the Greek equivalent of the powerful and comprehensive Hebrew word, *shalom*. *Shalom* means much more than the cessation of hostilities. It means the total well-being of people. Much more than freedom from conflict, its meaning includes fullness of days, health and happiness in home and community. It includes the notion of covenant union of a people with God and of those people individually with one another.

In Luke's Gospel "peace," as this plenitude of life, is the message that was preached by Jesus and is to be preached by the Church. In John's Gospel "peace" is seen not as the result of human efforts, but as a divine gift that flows from the resurrection. It is the risen Jesus who says: "*My* peace I give you. And it is not the kind that the world gives." Because he saw the alienation, aggression, and violence that existed in the world, peacemaking, for Paul, becomes "reconciliation." This is what he presents in second Corinthians as the whole meaning of Christ's coming: "God was in Christ reconciling the world to Himself" (19). It is also the mission of the Church and her members. In that same passage from the Corinthian Epistle, Paul tells us that the One who through Christ was reconciling the world to Himself "has given us the ministry of reconciliation" (5:18).

The "New Moment" Introduced by the Constantinian Age

This understanding of the Christian vocation, which rises out of an honest reading of the text, is — I think it is fair to say — the way that Christians saw their mission in the world for the first four centuries of the Christian era. The "just-war" doctrine did not develop in Christian thought till after the time of the Emperor Constantine (A.D. 312–337). When Constantine declared his support for Christianity and especially when, under the Emperor Theodosius (346–395), Christianity became the religion of the Empire, a "new moment," full of hope for the kingdom of God and yet fraught with dangers to that kingdom, came into being: Christians whose lives had been up to this time fundamentally "counter-culture" had to make new decisions, now that it was within their power to fashion the culture in which they would live. Entering into positions of influence in the affairs of state (where war was accepted as a normal way of settling disputes), Christians had to decide: Would they continue the nonviolent commitment of the first four centuries or would they accept war as a fact of life and limit their goals to trying to restrict as much as possible the ravages caused by war?

By and large, they chose the latter course, turning to a theory that had been developed by the Stoics and later by Cicero, namely, the doctrine that has come to be known as the "just-war" theory.

The Truce of God: An Experiment

It is fair to say, I think, that in a Christian context, the "just-war" theory was intended not so much to "justify" war as to limit the damages it could cause. It was a way of compromising with "necessity." If war had to be accepted as part of the human condition, then the task of the Church was to do all it could to restrict the ravages of war. Accepting the "just-war" doctrine was one way of doing this. Another was the experiment, organized chiefly by the monks of Cluny in the eleventh century, and known as the "truce of God." Encouraged by the monks of Cluny the bishops of Gaul, and then their brother-bishops of Italy, espoused this peace experiment, which eventually Pope Urban II (1088–1099) extended to the whole of Christendom. The appeal issued by the bishops of Provence in 1041, for instance, explains the meaning of the "truce of God"; it called on Christians to keep

> the peace and this truce of God which has been handed down to us from Heaven by Divine Mercy and which we have received and hold firmly. It consists in the fact that from the hour of Vespers on Wednesday there is to be firm peace among all Christians, friend or foe, and a truce, which shall last until sunrise on Monday morning.

Later other periods of abstinence from war were added, such as Advent, Christmastide, Lent, Eastertide, the Octave of Pentecost, certain feasts of the Blessed Virgin and other saints' feasts. (The above quotation and information taken from: Philip Contamine, *War in the Middle Ages*, trans. Michael Jones [Oxford, Blackwell, 1984], p. 272).

It is questionable whether or not the "truce of God" was ever observed for any length of time or with any consistency. And the whole arrangement may strike us as absurd or, at the very least, naïve. What sense did it make for Christians to "love" one another for four days and then turn about and kill one another for three days? And of course the answer is that it made absolutely no sense at all. And that may have been the precise intent of the monks of Cluny in promoting this "truce": to get people to see the absurdity of war, the absurdity of Christian men sharing the Lord's table on the Lord's Day and then lining up on opposite sides of a battlefield a day later. Peace, "firm peace," is not something that can be turned on and off. These monks were too attuned to the meaning of symbol not to see and want to help others see the frightful irrationality of a life claiming to be Christian that would choose to alternate loving with killing. Nor should we forget that, as monks, they would have been deeply committed to contemplation and to that contemplative understanding of people that would see their essential unity in God and, therefore, would of necessity view war as a wicked rending of that unity.

Despite efforts to limit war, it is a fact of history that Christians, who after Constantine achieved positions of prominence in world affairs, accommodated themselves to the existential situation that they found to be a part of the conduct of affairs of state and accepted war as a practical necessity. It is one of many instances where Christians have accommodated themselves quite readily to a *status quo* that the Gospel would seem to be calling them to oppose. At any rate, the pacifist, nonviolent, dimension of Christian faith was all but lost. There remained some few Christians who continued to believe that nonviolence was the only legitimate Christian stance. But the vast majority—Roman Catholics, supported by the Magisterium of their Church—chose to go the way of the "just-war" doctrine.

Earlier I made the point that a "new moment" came into being in human history in the fourth century when Christianity became the religion of the Roman Empire: a "moment," full of hope yet also fraught with danger, for the growth of the kingdom of God. In their 1983 pastoral letter entitled *The Challenge of Peace*, the bishops of the United States make use of the phrase "the new moment." They give the term a precise meaning. They intend it to designate the beginning of the nuclear age, which they view as a choice: either a *demonic* moment fraught with the danger of nuclear holocaust, or a *creative* moment summoning us to muster public opinion and to direct public policy in such a way that war may be relegated to the past of human history.

A New "New Moment"

I would like to suggest another possible way in which our age may be called a "new moment" in human history. It is a "new moment" in that the threat of nuclear annihilation seems to have been the catalyst that has enabled us to recover the tradition of nonviolence and pacifism that, for the most part, has lain dormant in the Christian (certainly the Roman Catholic) consciousness for fifteen hundred years. How far we have come in a short time is clear from the position taken by the Second Vatican Council in its document on the Church in the Modern World, *Gaudium et Spes* (no. 78): The bishops praise those who renounce the way of violence in defending their rights. That this stance was revolutionary (for Roman Catholics at least) is evident from the fact that it came only a decade after Pope Pius XII (d. 1958) had affirmed that a Catholic could not be a conscientious objector in war. A Catholic, he taught, could only object to a war that was manifestly unjust. And of course it is hardly conceivable that any nation would admit that it was involved in a war that was unjust.

The American bishops, in their pastoral letter *The Challenge of Peace*, built on the teaching of the Council and went further in accepting nonviolence. Speaking of the "just-war" doctrine and the commitment to nonviolence, the bishops see "these two distinct moral responses as having a complementary relationship, in the sense that both seek to serve the common good."

> They differ in their perception of how the common good is to be defended most effectively, but both responses testify to the Christian conviction that peace must be pursued and rights defended within moral restraints and in the context of defining other basic human values.

In fact, the bishops, in the resounding "No" that they say to nuclear war and in the firm agreement they express with the earnest desire articulated so strongly by Pope John Paul II that war be consigned to the past of human history, seem to suggest — so it seems to me at least — that those who believe in the theory of the "just war" have moved toward a conjunction of conclusion with those who hold to the commitment of nonviolence. What I mean is that more and more "just-war" people are realizing that modern warfare simply cannot meet the conditions laid down for a "just war." This means they are coming very close to saying that war today cannot be justified. Of course this has always been the stance of those who believe in the principle of nonviolence. For them war is always wrong, because the Gospel commits us to an unconditional love for our sisters and brothers that is simply incompatible with killing them.

It would be a mistake, however, to think that because many "just-war" people draw the same conclusion about war today, they are in the same position as the proponents of nonviolence. They are not in the same position, because the steps you take to arrive at a conclusion are in a very real sense a part of that conclusion. It would seem fair to say that at the present moment quite a number of "just-war" people are in a very uncomfortable position. Their principles have led them to a conclusion but cannot lead them beyond that conclusion. The point I want to make is that, once you have arrived, through application of the "just-war" principles, at the conclusion that modern warfare is immoral, these principles can give you no help in deciding what you do next. Their usefulness is exhausted in the conclusion. They have used up all their power, once they have shown that war cannot be justified. They cannot take you beyond that conclusion to a course of action that would follow from it.

Nonviolence as a Way of Life

It should be clear that this is not true of the nonviolent alternative. The efficacy of the principle of nonviolence is not exhausted in the conclusion that war is immoral. For the principle of nonviolence is concerned with much more than the issue of war. The conclusion that war is immoral is but one conclusion on a whole trajectory of conclusions that are concerned with the total way in which we live our lives. In other words, nonviolence does not exist to declare war wrong; it exists to declare unconditional love right. It is a call to commit my life ever more fully to that kind of love.

Unconditional love is a love that makes demands on oneself rather than on the other. It is a love that brooks no "if" clauses. It does not say: "I love you if you do this or if you avoid that." It simply says: "I love you regardless of what you do or say. I love you because no matter what you say or do you are the ikon, the image of God." The perception that is at the heart of unconditional love is the contemplative insight that says to the other: "You and I are one in God. This oneness is at a level of awareness that perhaps we do not achieve often enough, but it is there." In fact, contemplation really means saying to the "other": "There actually is no "other"; we are all one in God."

Unconditional love, then, is not just a stance about war. It is contemplation translated into the dynamism of everyday relationships. It helps me to understand in a whole new way what it means to be a person, what it means to be "in Christ," and what it means "to walk in the presence of the Lord in the land of the living." It is the "love-force" (*satyagraha*) that flows from the experience of contemplation.

There is a story (and I borrow it from my good friend, Jim Forest, without knowing where he found it) about a rabbi who was talking with his disciples about the difference between night and day. The question he put to his students was: "When can you know that the night has ended and the day has begun?" One disciple asked: "Is it the moment when you can tell the difference between a sheep and a dog?" "No," said the rabbi, "it isn't that." Another disciple tried: "Is it when you can see the difference between an olive tree and a fig tree?" "No," the rabbi answered, "it isn't that either." Then he looked deeply into the eyes of his disciples and said: "It is the moment when you look at a face you have never seen before and recognize the stranger as a brother or sister. Until that time comes," he added, "no matter how bright the day, it is still night for you."

It is a touching story. But we must take it even further. It is not enough to look into a face you have never seen before and recognize a brother or sister. We also have to be able to look into the faces of people we *have* seen before: perhaps seen with the eyes of anger or hatred or impatience or jealousy or ill will of any kind. To look into the face of such a person and see a brother or sister whom you really love with no strings attached — this is the meaning of unconditional love.

God: Contemplative and Nonviolent

God is supremely the contemplative One: He always *IS* in total awareness of all that is. God is supremely nonviolent. He lets His sun "rise on the bad and the good, He rains on the just and the unjust" (Matt. 5:45). He gives to each creature that which constitutes its identity and its uniqueness; and He never violates what He has given. Jesus Christ is the Contemplation and the Nonviolence of God made visible among us. When he calls us to be "perfect as our heavenly Father is perfect" (Matt. 5:48), he is, I should like to suggest, speaking about the perfection of contemplation and nonviolence. I am most like God when I am fully aware of reality as it truly is. I am most like God when I respect the dignity of every human person as inviolate, i.e., never to be violated, never to be the subject of violence.

Every time I ridicule another person, put someone down, talk about him or her, broadcast a person's faults—I am being a violent person. Every time I speak the unkind word, the cutting word, the word that carelessly or wantonly bares another's wounds—I am being violent. And when I am violent, I have turned daylight into darkness. I have turned off the brightness of the power of love.

Jesus and Nonviolence

The greatness of nonviolence consists in this: It releases the greatest healing, purifying, unifying power in all the world. This is what Jesus did in his life and especially in his death. He refused to fight violence with violence. He had only one weapon: love. That is why he told Peter—the disciple who wanted to fight it out in the Garden of Gethsemane—to put back his sword. Those who live by the sword, he said, will perish by the sword. My Father, he told Peter, could furnish legions of angels who could vanquish with a glance all who come against me. But my Father did not send me to win over people, but to win people over—through the power of unconditional love.

This does not mean that Jesus did not resist evil. (It is a common misunderstanding to see nonviolence as a weakness whereby you allow people to do whatever they want to you rather than seeing it for what it really is: confronting the other with the truth, having confidence in the inherent power of the truth and seeking the truth that can be discovered in the "adversary".) Jesus resisted those who betrayed and oppressed the poor. He resisted those who profaned the Temple. He resisted those who struck him on the cheek. But *he resisted in a nonviolent way. He refused to allow people to make him hate them.* He refused to allow anything to make him forget that inviolable dignity that is God's gift to every human person. His most unforgettable words are the prayer he cried out from the cross to his Father on behalf of those who had so wrongfully oppressed him: "Father, forgive them, for they do not know what they are doing." Surely it was the noblest moment of nonviolence in the pages of human history.

Contemplation and nonviolence are two sides of the same coin. Let them into your life and you had better be prepared to see things happen to you you would never have dreamed of. The contemplation-nonviolence syndrome is a *metanoia* so profound that it brings astounding changes into one's life. Certainly I am not the best one to assess to what degree I have absorbed the intuition of contemplation and been moved by the dynamism of nonviolence. I do know this: that, if for many years I have been fighting against this intuition and that dynamism, I'm losing the battle and they seem to be getting the upper hand. Changes are taking place in my life. I believe that, at long last, I am becoming much more tolerant of people, more sympathetic to their needs, more sensitive to the way I treat them (and as I write this, I am wondering if maybe there are a dozen people ready to shout: "No, you aren't!").

One event that happened in my life and that made the word "grace" seem more real to me than anything I had ever experienced before took place on October 23, 1983. It's a day I shall never forget. It was a Sunday and I had just finished presiding at a Eucharistic liturgy. As I was returning to my office, someone told me: "Something terrible has just taken place: over two hundred and fifty marines were killed by a suicide terrorist attack in Beirut." My reaction was instantaneous. Strangely, it was not, first of all, compassion or distress or anger. No, the thought that flashed into my mind seemed to have no connection whatsoever with the terrible massacre that had occurred.

What came to my mind was: "I shall never smoke again." I had been a moderately heavy smoker and had smoked for over forty years.

Why did that thought seem, for a brief time at least, to crowd out all other more appropriate reactions? I do not know. All I can surmise is that a process of intuition went on in my mind over which it seemed I had no control and to which I gave no direction. It was as if I was "reasoning" (though I went through no reasoning process at all): "This was a heinous act of violence. I want to make some immediate protest against this violence. There is one thing I can do immediately: I can cease doing the violence to my own body that smoking involves. I shall never smoke again."

I am writing about this several years after the event. I have never smoked since that day nor have I had any desire to do so. And not even for a day did I experience any "withdrawal symptoms," even though I had obviously had a strong addiction to tobacco. This may sound quite insignificant and, compared to the event that precipitated it, it certainly pales in importance. Yet to this day I feel that this moment several years ago was, as I have already said, one of the most palpable moments of grace that I have ever experienced.

A moment of "grace" described may not seem as moving as such a moment actually experienced. All I know is that a number of things going on in my life at that time helped prepare me for the grace of that moment: reflecting on some of the "hard" passages in the Gospels about loving the neighbor, reading what Thomas Merton, speaking out of a contemplative context, had to say about nonviolence, meeting with some of the people who were his friends (people like Jim Forest and Jim Douglass and most especially Hildegard Goss-Mayr), visiting the women's encampment at the Seneca Depot near Rochester, New York, where almost certainly nuclear weapons are stored—all these prepared me for a special moment of grace. But more than that, they have convinced me that nonviolence as a way of life is not an option for me but a choice that I must make.

What this means for me I am not sure. I know it means that I must oppose all war and must be committed to total disarmament. It also obliges me to resist evil in every way that I can, yet without ever resorting to ways that are violent. I know too that it has a great deal to say about how I am obligated to act toward other people. I shall know that I am truly committed to nonviolent love only when it becomes not just an attitude toward war, but a way of life that will somehow affect everything I do.

People climb ladders to get to high places they would not otherwise be able to reach. Contemplation and nonviolence are lofty goals worth striving for. There may be a number of ways of reaching these goals. What this book has tried to show is that one of these ways that has had credibility for a long time is Guigo's ladder—and I want to add Gandhi's too. I link him with Guigo because, while centuries separate the two of them, the unity of the human spirit links them in their search for goals that have always challenged the highest reachings of the human spirit.

Perhaps all that remains to be said is that this journey up the ladder—a ladder that is located not really in space but in the human heart—helps lift us above our so many illusions about what is real in life. Thus, the climb—which in reality turns out to be no climb at all—can help remove the veils that prevent us from seeing the Face of Him who is Invisible.

Select Bibliography

Burrows, Ruth. *Ascent to Love: The Spiritual Teaching of St John of the Cross*. London: Darton, Longman and Todd, 1987.

Finely, James. *Merton's Palace of Nowhere*. Notre Dame, IN: Ave Maria Press, 1978.

Finley, Mitch. *Catholic Spiritual Classics*. Kansas City: Sheed and Ward, 1987.

Gatta, Julia. *Julian of Norwich, The Cloud of Unknowing, Walter Hilton: Three Spiritual Directors for Our Time*. Cambridge, MA: Cowley Publications, 1986.

Guigo II. *The Ladder of Monks and Twelve Meditations*. Translated by Edmund Colledge and James Walsh. Kalamazoo, MI: Cistercian Publications, 1981. Previously available in Doubleday Image Books.

Johnston, William. *Christian Zen*. San Francisco: Harper and Row, 1971.

Keating, Thomas. *Open Mind, Open Heart*. Amity, NY: Amity House, 1986.

Le Saux, Henri, O. S. B. (Abishiktananda). *Prayer*. Philadelphia: Westminster Press, 1967.

_____. *Saccidananda: A Christian Approach to Advaitic Experience*. Delhi, India: ISPSK, 1974.

Merton, Thomas. *The Asian Journal of Thomas Merton*. Edited by Naomi Burton, Brother Patrick Hart, and James Laughlin, with Amiya Chakravarty as consulting editor. New York: New Directions, 1973.

_____. *The Climate of Monastic Prayer*. Spencer, MA: Cistercian Publications, 1969. Also published by Herder and Herder under the title *Contemplative Prayer*.

_____. *Contemplation in a World of Action*. New York: Doubleday, 1971.

_____. *Disputed Questions*. New York: Farrar, Straus and Giroux, 1960. Especially "The Philosophy of Solitude," pp. 177–207.

_____. *The Hidden Ground of Love: Letters on Religious Experience and Social Concerns*. Edited by William H. Shannon. New York: Farrar, Straus and Giroux, 1985 (paperback 1986).

_____. Holograph Journals: Notebooks nos. 18, 28, 43. Thomas Merton Studies Center, Louisville, KY.

_____. *Introductions East and West*: The Foreign Prefaces of Thomas Merton. Edited by Robert E. Daggy. Greensboro, NC: Unicorn Press, 1979.

_____. *Mystics and Zen Masters*. New York: Farrar, Straus and Giroux, 1967.

_____. *New Seeds of Contemplation*. New York: New Directions, 1962.

_____. *The Non-Violent Alternative*. Edited by Gordon Zahn. New York: Farrar, Straus and Giroux, 1980.

_____. *Thoughts in Solitude*. New York: Farrar, Straus and Giroux, 1958.

Shannon, William H. *Thomas Merton's Dark Path*. Revised edition. New York: Farrar, Straus and Giroux, 1987.